Pause *and* Pray

Pause
and
Pray

180 Encouraging
Devotional Prayers
for Teen Girls

BARBOUR
PUBLISHING

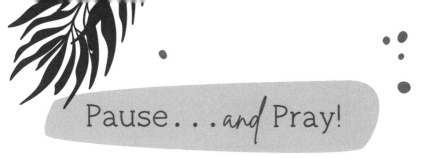

Pause...and Pray!

Devote yourselves to prayer,
being watchful and thankful.
COLOSSIANS 4:2 NIV

· ·

The all-powerful God cares deeply for you, even in the day-to-day details of your life. In fact, He longs to hear from you. You are invited—any time and for any reason—to bring prayers to the King of the universe. Now that's genuine love!

The prayers in this book will help you develop a more intimate relationship with your Father God. As you read the devotional prayers, make them your own. Meditate on the scriptures. You may even wish to keep a journal on hand to record your personal thoughts as you reflect upon God's amazing love for you.

You will be blessed when you pause and pray!

Choosing Contentment

*I have learned in whatever situation I am to
be content. I know how to be brought low,
and I know how to abound. In any and every
circumstance, I have learned the secret of facing
plenty and hunger, abundance and need. I can
do all things through him who strengthens me.*
PHILIPPIANS 4:11–13 ESV

• •

Father, the culture around me insists that I deserve
more food, more fashion, more entertainment, more
pleasure. But when I agree, when I scramble after
more and more, I always end up feeling empty. You
offer another way. And when I choose contentment,
when I choose gratitude, when I choose to joyfully
receive what You have given, then I am finally *full*.
Teach me to choose contentment in every situation,
for Your glory and for my good. Amen.

God Protects Me from Evil

My prayer is not that you take them out of the world but that you protect them from the evil one.
JOHN 17:15 NIV

Father God, I am blessed when I eavesdrop on the very prayers that Jesus prayed for His followers—that Jesus prayed for me! And I hear that He didn't pray that my life would be easy. Or that I would be rich. Or that I'd never struggle. Or that I'd never fail. Jesus prayed that *You would protect me* from the evil one. God, that is my prayer today as well. By Your grace, I reject the lies of my adversary. Help me to recognize his wily schemes, and strengthen me by the power of Your Word and Your Spirit. I am confident that You are my good Protector, in Jesus' name. Amen.

Guarding My Mind

You will keep in perfect peace those whose minds are steadfast, because they trust in you.
ISAIAH 26:3 NIV

. . . .

As I spend time with You, Lord, I learn to trust You. Your Word is my weapon to fight negative thoughts. I will be careful about the things I see and hear because I know they can affect my thinking. Help me guard my mind. Help me focus on the truth so that no negative thought will have power over me.

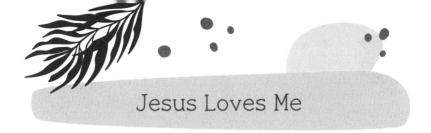

Jesus Loves Me

I pray that you, being rooted and established in love, may have power, together with all the Lord's holy people, to grasp how wide and long and high and deep is the love of Christ, and to know this love that surpasses knowledge—that you may be filled to the measure of all the fullness of God.
EPHESIANS 3:17–19 NIV

. . . .

Father God, Your love is amazing. And Jesus' love for me is beyond what I can even wrap my brain around. Jesus loves me. Me! I don't need to do anything on my own to earn that love. All I need is to believe in Him and accept His love as a beautiful gift. Day by day, moment by moment, please give me power to begin to grasp how wide and long and high and deep Christ's love is for me. It's a marvelous thing that can transform every part of my life. In Jesus' name I pray, amen.

God Revives My Heart

Create in me a pure heart, O God, and renew a steadfast spirit within me. Do not cast me from your presence or take your Holy Spirit from me. Restore to me the joy of your salvation and grant me a willing spirit, to sustain me.
PSALM 51:10–12 NIV

God, I thank You that You know my heart. You know when I'm soaring high: after receiving good news, or doing great on a test, or winning an award, or surprising a friend. And You know when my heart is low: when my emotions are low, or when I've been disappointed, or when I've sinned. You know my heart, and You promise to renew and revive it. God, allow Your Spirit to move within me so my heart may be pure and I may rejoice in You. Amen.

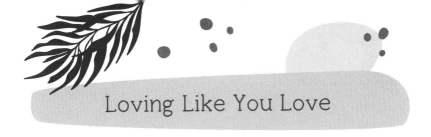

Loving Like You Love

"A new command I give you: Love one another.
As I have loved you, so you must love one
another. By this everyone will know that you
are my disciples, if you love one another."
JOHN 13:34–35 NIV

. . . .

Jesus, I hear the words You spoke to Your first followers and the words You speak to me: *Love one another.* I confess that although I long to live faithfully, my flesh gets in the way of me loving my family, loving my friends, and loving the world that You love. But You've shown me what love looks like. I learn how to love when I peek into the Gospels and see how You loved rich and poor, adults and children, saints and sinners, male and female, Jews and those who weren't Jewish. And because You equip me, I commit to loving others with Your love today. Amen.

Giving My Thoughts to God

*Whatever things are true, whatever things
are noble, whatever things are just, whatever
things are pure, whatever things are lovely,
whatever things are of good report, if there
is any virtue and if there is anything
praiseworthy—meditate on these things.*

PHILIPPIANS 4:8 NKJV

. . . .

Lord, I confess that I am tempted to think about things
that don't help me grow to be more like Jesus. Whether
it's the music I put in my ears, the shows and movies I
watch with my eyes, or even the ways that my imagi-
nation can get away from me, I know I need Your help.
This week, when I notice thoughts that don't honor
You, help me replace them with all that is true, honest,
just, pure, lovely, and good. Thank You for being my
Helper. Amen.

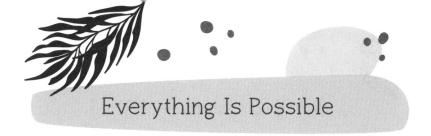

Everything Is Possible

"Abba, Father, all things are possible for You."
MARK 14:36 NKJV

How amazing! You, my Father, are the Creator of the universe! Your infinite creativity formed everything, everywhere. I know I can trust in Your might and Your abilities; there's nothing in heaven or on earth that You can't handle. Forgive me when I try to take things into my own hands. Since You made the world, I know You can take care of my small life!

Doing Good in Secret

"Don't do your good deeds publicly, to be admired by others, for you will lose the reward from your Father in heaven."
MATTHEW 6:1 NLT

. . . .

You know my heart, Lord. You know that I long to live a life that is pleasing to You. And You also know that I struggle against the natural human temptation to let others know what I'm up to: to be sure they see me bowing my head before a meal, to mention the child I sponsor overseas, or to point out the ways I've served in my community. You know that's not who I want to be. So I commit to keeping quiet about the good I do, to keeping it just between You and me. Our secret! Cleanse my heart so that I might love and serve You well. Amen.

Stop Striving

"Be still, and know that I am God."
PSALM 46:10 ESV

· ·

Father, I come to You weighed down by my busyness. So much is going on in my life, and I feel like I'm cramming so much into my days. I know I don't have to do all the things to make You love me. In fact, Your Word tells me to be still and know You are God. That means I need to stop striving. I admit it feels almost impossible to be still. It's hard to not strive, and it feels like everything in this world is so far from being still. Yet tonight, as I draw close to You, I choose to quiet my heart. I want to take this time to be still with You. In this quiet place, please help me to know You are God. In Jesus' name I pray, amen.

Uniquely Gifted

*If the whole body were an eye, where would be
the sense of hearing? If the whole body were
an ear, where would be the sense of smell?
But as it is, God arranged the members in
the body, each one of them, as he chose.*
1 CORINTHIANS 12:17–18 ESV

Father, sometimes when I look at the gifts others have, I feel jealous. I notice the creativity that she has. Or the writing gifts he has. Or the athletic skill she has. But I trust that You have given gifts exactly as You have chosen. And I am confident that You have equipped me with all I need to serve as a member of Your body. Lord, I commit all that I have and all that I am to You and to Your kingdom. Amen.

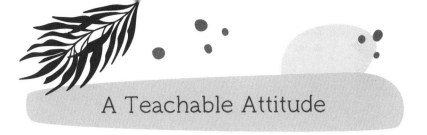

A Teachable Attitude

Listen to my words. Turn your ear to my sayings. . . . Keep them in the center of your heart. For they are life to those who find them.
PROVERBS 4:20–22 NLV

. . . .

Holy Spirit, be my Teacher. Guide me as I read the Bible. Show me how to let go of any selfishness or stubbornness and listen to Your direction. I'll go where You want me to go today. Help me focus my heart and energy on Your instruction.

Living as One Who's Accepted

Jesus said to her, "I who speak to you am he." . . .
*So the woman left her water jar and went
away into town and said to the people,
"Come, see a man who told me all that
I ever did. Can this be the Christ?"*
JOHN 4:26, 28–29 ESV

. . . .

Lord, sometimes I fear that if people really knew me—if they knew my history, my thoughts, and my fears—they would reject me. So I show the world the version of me I think they'll accept. But inside I'm hungry to be received and loved exactly as I am. I see Your generous face smiling upon a woman who was rejected in her community. And I see You smiling upon me. Lord, fill me with Your gracious presence so I can live as one who is known and loved by You. Amen.

A New Mind

Don't copy the behavior and customs of this world, but let God transform you into a new person by changing the way you think. Then you will learn to know God's will for you, which is good and pleasing and perfect.

ROMANS 12:2 NLT

. . . .

God who created my mind and all that I am, I offer myself to You. Daily my thoughts are influenced by the world's loud messages that I see and hear in advertisements, television shows, songs, movies, and even in what my friends post on social media. But I thank You that You're at work renewing my mind to embrace a new way of thinking. And thank You for the confidence that, by Your Spirit, I can know what is good. I can know what pleases You. I can know what is perfect. Lord, guide my thoughts and decisions today. Amen.

Receiving Jesus

Yet to all who did receive him, to those who believed in his name, he gave the right to become children of God.
<small>JOHN 1:12 NIV</small>

· ·

Lord, I believe in Your name. Help me believe even more. Take away the doubts that the world shouts at me every day. Keep my eyes focused on You, even when troubles come. Keep my ears tuned to Your voice, especially when I'm tempted to listen to other voices. I welcome You into my heart.

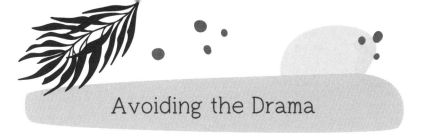

Avoiding the Drama

Have nothing to do with foolish, ignorant controversies; you know that they breed quarrels. And the Lord's servant must not be quarrelsome but kind to everyone, able to teach, patiently enduring evil, correcting his opponents with gentleness. God may perhaps grant them repentance leading to a knowledge of the truth.
2 Timothy 2:23–25 esv

. . . .

Lord, You know the foolishness that gets stirred up among people: this comment on social media, that social slight, this accusation, or that gossip. And it's so easy to get sucked into the drama! Father, I want to live differently, as one who shines Your light in the world—at home, at school, at church, and in the world. Help me exercise wisdom and avoid useless controversies. I trust You to be my Helper as I show others Your kindness. Amen.

No Worries

Humble yourselves, therefore, under God's mighty hand, that he may lift you up in due time. Cast all your anxiety on him because he cares for you.
1 PETER 5:6–7 NIV

• •

Father, knowing that You care for me changes my life. I'm so glad You love me and that I matter to You. And I'm so thankful I can tell You all of my cares and worries. I know You'll listen to me and help. So many things feel like burdens right now. They're weighing me down. But I choose to surrender them to You. I know I can't handle all that I'm facing and feeling, but I know You can. You're mighty enough to do more than I can even imagine. I trust You'll work out all the details. When I'm tempted to feel anxious, please replace all of my worry with peace. Please help me trust You completely and rest in that trust. In Jesus' name I pray, amen.

God of Power and Surprise

When Pharaoh's horses, chariots and horsemen
went into the sea, the LORD brought the waters
of the sea back over them, but the Israelites
walked through the sea on dry ground.
EXODUS 15:19 NIV

When Your people who were oppressed as slaves in Egypt cried out to You, You heard their pleas. And when You called them out of bondage, Lord, You went *big*. When they fled—without weapons, without protection, without provision—You defended them and toppled the warriors who pursued them. In a mighty act of power that no one saw coming, You rescued Your people. God, I'm convinced that You are the same all-merciful, all-powerful Savior today. I see how You make a way where it seems there isn't one, and so I'm willing to trust You with the big stuff in my life because You can do all things. Amen.

Showing Mercy

*Never pay back someone for the bad
he has done to you. Let the anger of
God take care of the other person.*
ROMANS 12:19 NLV

· ·

Lord, when others treat me unfairly, judge me, or take
something I feel I deserved, I want to get even. I want
to fight for what is mine, but then I feel You urging
me to choose a different response. Showing mercy is
difficult sometimes, but with Your love and grace, I can.

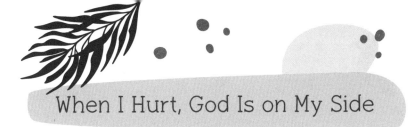

When I Hurt, God Is on My Side

You keep track of all my sorrows. You have collected all my tears in your bottle. You have recorded each one in your book. My enemies will retreat when I call to you for help. This I know: God is on my side!
PSALM 56:8–9 NLT

. . . .

Lord, You know the hurts—the little ones and the big ones—that I hold in my heart. You've kept track of every bruise, bump, and tear. And although the deceiver hisses that You do not care for me, I am convinced that You are on my side. I am comforted by Your presence and grateful for Your care. God, thank You for receiving all of me, even my tender places. Amen.

Giving God My Gifts

*He and all his companions were astonished
at the catch of fish they had taken, and so
were James and John, the sons of Zebedee,
Simon's partners. Then Jesus said to Simon,
"Don't be afraid; from now on you will fish
for people." So they pulled their boats up on
shore, left everything and followed him.*
LUKE 5:9–11 NIV

When I witness the way Jesus engaged and called a band of fishermen at the seashore, I notice a restlessness in my own heart to follow You. You took what these men had—the ability to fish—and redeemed it for the good of Your kingdom. Lord, today I offer You my own gifts—my creativity, my physical strength, my intellect, my generosity, my problem-solving skills, everything You've given me—and I ask You to use me. Speak, Lord, Your servant is listening. Amen.

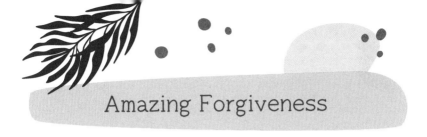

Amazing Forgiveness

*In Him we have redemption through
His blood, the forgiveness of sins,
according to the riches of His grace.*
EPHESIANS 1:7 NKJV

• •

Lord, thank You for forgiveness. Many people struggle with guilt because of what they've done in the past, but I know my past is redeemed because of Christ's sacrifice for me. Your forgiveness is so amazing! Even though I don't deserve it, You pour it out freely and lovingly. Because You have chosen to pardon me, I bless Your name today.

More Than Skin-Deep

But the LORD said to Samuel, "Do not consider his appearance or his height, for I have rejected him. The LORD does not look at the things people look at. People look at the outward appearance, but the LORD looks at the heart."
1 SAMUEL 16:7 NIV

. . . .

Father God, I admit it's hard to *not* focus on appearances. It feels natural to judge my looks. I don't always like what I see, even though You created me and You see what's inside of me. It's also really hard to not judge other people by what they look like. I know I shouldn't, but I do. Please help me see what's really inside others so I can make wise choices about my friends. Please open my eyes to see people who need You—and help me to reach out to them, especially if I normally wouldn't want to talk with them. Please help me look deeper than just the surface level. In Jesus' name I pray, amen.

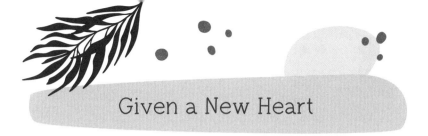

Given a New Heart

"I will give you a new heart, and a new spirit I will put within you. And I will remove the heart of stone from your flesh and give you a heart of flesh."
<small>EZEKIEL 36:26 ESV</small>

Lord, You promise that You are removing my heart of stone and giving me a new heart and a new spirit. This is what I need! My heart is hard because I've chosen to disobey what I know is right. My heart is hard from the times I've ignored Your voice. And my heart is also hard from the defenses I've put up to protect myself from getting hurt by others. Because I believe that You can be trusted with my heart, I offer it to You, the Good Physician, and I welcome the new heart You are knitting together inside me. Amen.

Strength in God

*The LORD is my strength and shield.
I trust him with all my heart. He helps
me, and my heart is filled with joy.*
PSALM 28:7 NLT

• •

Lord, You are my strength and my shield. You give me courage to meet challenges. You build me up, leading me to places I never would have dreamed possible. You are the Friend who never leaves me, the Guide who walks ahead of me. With You in my life, I can do anything.

Committed to Purity

How can a young person stay on the path of purity? By living according to your word. I seek you with all my heart; do not let me stray from your commands. I have hidden your word in my heart that I might not sin against you.
PSALM 119:9–11 NIV

God, You know exactly what I'm up against as I commit myself to live faithfully to You. You know what other students are talking about and what they're doing on weekends. You know how culture bombards me with temptations. And You know how I can be tempted to rationalize my words and actions. God, I am seeking You with my whole heart. I believe Your Word strengthens and empowers me to avoid sin. Be my helper today. Amen.

Offering My Hurts to God

Do not say, "I'll pay you back for this wrong!"
Wait for the LORD, and he will avenge you.
PROVERBS 20:22 NIV

· ·

Faithful God, thank You that I can trust You with the most tender matters of the heart. You know the ways that I have been bumped, bruised, and battered throughout my life. And You know the hearts of those who've wronged me. I admit that it's tempting to want to respond in anger, to speak unkind words, and to even the score by returning wrong for wrong. But I hear Your voice of wisdom calming my heart, inviting me to trust You. God, I offer You the hurts I've received from others. I release them into Your keeping so I don't have to carry them anymore. Thank You for Your mercy and Your care for me. Amen.

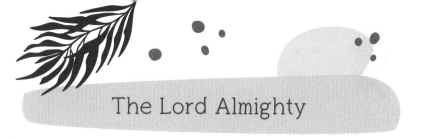

The Lord Almighty

"I will be a Father to you. You will be My sons and daughters, says the All-powerful God."
2 CORINTHIANS 6:18 NLV

• •

You, Lord God, can do all things for You are almighty and ever-present. Because You are my Father, I know I can trust You to handle every part of my life. I trust You with my past, my present, and my future. You are God, and I'm not—and I'm thankful that's the way it is.

Loving Enemies

"Love your enemies! Do good to them. Lend to them without expecting to be repaid. Then your reward from heaven will be very great, and you will truly be acting as children of the Most High."

LUKE 6:35 NLT

. . . .

Dear God, I have a hard time loving some of the people in my life. But You ask me to be kind to my enemies—to do good things for them without thinking about what I'll get back. Not easy! Please help me obey.

Tomorrow

Yet you do not know what your life will be like tomorrow. You are just a vapor that appears for a little while and then vanishes away.
JAMES 4:14 NASB

. . . .

Lord, it's hard for me to remember that the worries and troubles of today won't last forever. I don't know what tomorrow will hold. I kind of wish I did. But I'm choosing to trust You. And as much as I wonder what will happen tomorrow—or next week or next month or next year—I don't have to worry. I know You're in control, and You have a wonderful plan. Even if it doesn't always feel like it, life is so short. Please help me make the most of every day. Especially my not-so-great days! Instead of getting discouraged or frustrated when things don't go my way, please help me to see You at work and trust You more and more. In Jesus' name I pray, amen.

Giving Back to God

Remember this: Whoever sows sparingly will also reap sparingly, and whoever sows generously will also reap generously. Each of you should give what you have decided in your heart to give, not reluctantly or under compulsion, for God loves a cheerful giver.
2 CORINTHIANS 9:6–7 NIV

God, when I hear Your call to give, I want to believe that it is for other people. But I know that You are inviting *me* to give joyfully to You, for the work of Your kingdom. I don't have a lot of money, but I offer You a portion of what You've given me. Show me how You would have me use that faithfully. And I also offer You my time and energy. Show me how You're calling me to use the particular gifts You've given me to build Your kingdom. All I have belongs to You. Amen.

Go to God

*This is the word that came to Jeremiah from
the LORD: "Go down to the potter's house,
and there I will give you my message."*
JEREMIAH 18:1–2 NIV

· ·

So many times, Lord, I feel like dropping to my knees
and praying but don't. Thank You that You keep calling
my name again and again. Please help me trust You
enough to stop what I'm doing when I hear Your call.
I'm on my knees now, Lord. I'm listening to Your voice.

Obeying My Father in Heaven

He replied to him, "Who is my mother, and who are my brothers?" Pointing to his disciples, he said, "Here are my mother and my brothers. For whoever does the will of my Father in heaven is my brother and sister and mother."
MATTHEW 12:48–50 NIV

God, I am convinced that loving my family well is one of my foremost assignments from You. So I'm on it. Help me to love them well. I'm also aware that my first allegiance is not to members of my family— especially when they do not know You, love You, or obey You—but it is to You. Father God, in life and in death, I belong to You. As I seek to live a life of love, one that is faithful to You, be my number one priority and Lord. Amen.

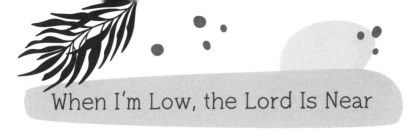

When I'm Low, the Lord Is Near

*The LORD is close to the brokenhearted and
saves those who are crushed in spirit.*
PSALM 34:18 NIV

God, I thank You that You know me inside and out.
You know the days when I'm flying high, full of joy
and life. And You know the days when I struggle to
keep it together. On those days when it's hard to get
out of bed, when I'm feeling crushed, I trust that You
are with me. When it feels like no one else gets it, Your
Word promises me that You are ready to help. God,
open my eyes today to see Your face shining upon me.
Thank You for being near and for holding me in Your
care when I feel so alone. Amen.

My Mouth and My Heart

*If you confess with your mouth Jesus as Lord, and
believe in your heart that God raised Him from
the dead, you will be saved; for with the heart a
person believes, resulting in righteousness, and
with the mouth he confesses, resulting in salvation.*
ROMANS 10:9–10 NASB

. . . .

Jesus, I do confess that You are Lord! And I truly believe in my heart of hearts that God raised You from the dead and that You're living right now. Thank You that You save me when I confess in faith that You're my Lord. And thank You that as I believe in You, You make me right with You. Being saved and being made right—salvation and righteousness—are such huge things I could never accomplish on my own. Thank You for taking care of both of them for me and choosing to give both salvation and righteousness to me. You are so very good! In Your name I pray, amen.

Authenticity

*"These people honor me with their lips,
but their hearts are far from me."*
MATTHEW 15:8 NIV

· ·

Lord, I want my heart and my actions to line up. The
things I do shouldn't be for attention or praise. Please
open my eyes to my real motivation when I decide to
do something. Keep me honest with myself and You.
Remind me that I represent You in the choices I make.
In everything, help me honor You from my heart.

God Is Working for Good

We know that in all things God works for the good of those who love him, who have been called according to his purpose.

Lord, when I look at some of the painful or difficult situations in my home, in my larger family, in my community, and in Your world, it is sometimes hard to find hope. When I see the ways that so many suffer, it's difficult to find meaning in the chaos. But Your Word reminds me that I don't see all that You see. I trust Your promise to work behind the scenes for the good of those who've been called by You and who love You. God, although I can't make sense of all I see, I put my trust in You today because You are good and You are faithful. Amen.

Speaking Up

If you remain silent at this time, relief and deliverance for the Jews will arise from another place, but you and your father's family will perish. And who knows but that you have come to your royal position for such a time as this?
ESTHER 4:14 NIV

When You chose Esther, Lord, You picked someone wildly unlikely to influence her culture. She was the wrong gender, wrong race, wrong religion. And yet when You gave her a big assignment, to speak truth to power, she said *yes*. She was brave. She was bold. She was faithful to You. God, I believe that You call unlikely young women today to speak bravely and boldly about what is wrong in our world. Give me Your courage to be faithful to You by telling the truth in love. Amen.

God's Word Is Truth

Jesus said, "If you hold to my teaching,
you are really my disciples. Then you will
know the truth, and the truth will set you free."
JOHN 8:31–32 NIV

• •

Lord, Your Word is true. I want to know the truth and live it. Help me look to Your solid Word, not to this world, for my life instruction manual. Thank You that You will never lead me off course, that You never lie to me, and that You always keep Your promises.

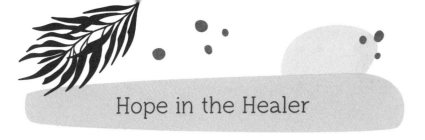

Hope in the Healer

A woman who had suffered from a discharge of blood for twelve years came up behind him and touched the fringe of his garment, for she said to herself, "If I only touch his garment, I will be made well." Jesus turned, and seeing her he said, "Take heart, daughter; your faith has made you well."
MATTHEW 9:20–22 ESV

Lord, I can't imagine what it would be like to bleed for twelve years. This woman You touched, who'd been ostracized by her community for being "unclean," must have been so weak physically, emotionally, and spiritually. She had hope in You, and You healed her. Lord, give me faith like this woman's. I offer You my tender broken places with the confidence that You care for me. Amen.

Using Words for Good

A gentle answer turns away wrath,
but a harsh word stirs up anger.
PROVERBS 15:1 NIV

Lord, although I want to honor You in all I do, I confess that this is difficult when anger bubbles up inside me. When someone messes with me at school, when they say things that aren't true, when my siblings annoy me, and when I disagree strongly with my parents, I want to lash out in anger. But Your Word challenges me to choose my response, my volume, and my tone carefully. My words have power—either to fuel a fire of angry rage or to de-escalate conflicts. God, help me use the power of my tongue for good, using my voice to turn away wrath and sow seeds of peace. Amen.

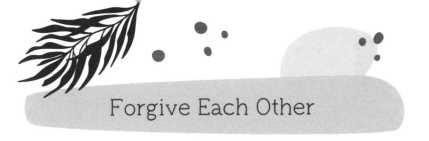

Forgive Each Other

Get rid of all bitterness, rage and anger, brawling
and slander, along with every form of malice.
EPHESIANS 4:31 NIV

Lord, forgiveness can be so hard sometimes. I need Your help to get rid of bitterness and anger. Help me build others up instead of putting them down—even when it seems like they deserve it. Teach me grace. Help me to forgive other people quickly and to be kind and compassionate, because I know Christ forgave all of us.

A Father's Mercy

I will be his Father, and he shall be My son;
and I will not take My mercy away from him.
1 CHRONICLES 17:13 NKJV

Thank You, Lord, for never taking Your mercy away from me. No matter how many times I let You down, I can always count on You to pick me up. I don't understand this gift, but I'm thankful for it. Please show me ways to extend mercy to the people in my life.

Speak Up!

Speak up for those who cannot speak for themselves, for the rights of all who are destitute. Speak up and judge fairly; defend the rights of the poor and needy.
PROVERBS 31:8–9 NIV

. . . .

Father God, thank You for giving me a voice! You've given me thoughts and words not only to express my feelings but also to speak up for others. Please use me to help other people, even if it seems awkward or uncomfortable. Please work on my heart so I have more compassion for people around me. Open my eyes so I can see who needs help. I want to do what's right and defend people who have a hard time defending themselves. I pray I'll be a kind friend to other teens who are left out. Please help me include outsiders and treat everyone with kindness, no matter what they look like, sound like, or what they can or cannot do. I'm trusting that You'll use me in a big way in someone else's life. In Jesus' name I pray, amen.

Convinced that God Is for Me

What, then, shall we say in response to these things? If God is for us, who can be against us?
ROMANS 8:31 NIV

. . . .

Faithful God, it is obvious that what we experience in this world is often not Your will. Children go hungry. They get sick. They endure abuse. Adults argue. They lose their jobs. They leave their homes and families. Communities fail to care for those in need, and nations wage war. God, I don't know how to make sense of such suffering. But in the midst of the chaos, whether in my life or in the world, I am certain of one thing: You are *for* me. No matter what I face, I have the confidence that You see, You care, and *You are for me.* Amen.

Light for Understanding

Your word is a lamp for my feet,
a light on my path.
PSALM 119:105 NIV

. . . .

Lord, Your Word is like a beam of light on my path through life, helping me see the way. Your words give me insight and hope even when I can't see where I'm going or how things will turn out. I'm so glad You know the right direction. You go ahead of me, so I don't need to be afraid. I choose to follow You.

Spending Myself for Others

*"If you do away with the yoke of oppression,
with the pointing finger and malicious talk, and if
you spend yourselves in behalf of the hungry and
satisfy the needs of the oppressed, then your light
will rise in the darkness, and your night will become
like the noonday. The LORD will guide you always."*
ISAIAH 58:9–11 NIV

· ·

God, You have made plain what delights Your heart. And You've promised that when we care for the most vulnerable, You are pleased and Your favor is with us. Lord, help me to be a faithful servant who loves You by loving others. Open my eyes this week to notice those who are hungry and those who are oppressed—both those who walk the halls at school with me and those around the globe who are known intimately by You. Equip me to respond faithfully, in Jesus' name. Amen.

My Body Is Good

You created my inmost being; you knit me together in my mother's womb. I praise you because I am fearfully and wonderfully made; your works are wonderful, I know that full well.

Creator God, You lovingly created the world, and I believe that includes *me*! I was not an accident. When I was in my mother's womb, You knit me together: my hair, my skin, my eyes, my nose, my frame. You saw Your handiwork, and You called it *good*. You call *me* good. Because You are my Maker, I ignore the voices swirling around me that insist I'm too tall or too short, too light or too dark, too fat or too thin. Instead I turn my eyes toward Your smiling face. I bend my ear toward Your voice, which confirms that I am fearfully and wonderfully made. I trust in what You say about me today. Amen.

Constant Praise

Be full of joy all the time. Never stop praying.
1 THESSALONIANS 5:16–17 NLV

• •

Lord, You've given me life, and I praise You. You've filled my lungs with air from my very first breath, and I praise You. I praise You because I am fearfully and wonderfully made. Today, Lord, I want to pray to You like I breathe: in and out, all day long. Fill my mouth with words that praise You. Let my lips shout how great You are.

A Life of Kindness

Whoever pursues righteousness and kindness
will find life, righteousness, and honor.
PROVERBS 21:21 ESV

Heavenly Father, it's so interesting that, just like believers should be known for their love, if I pursue kindness—a very loving trait—I'll find life. I pray that I'll seek and find a life of love and kindness. I want to be right in Your eyes. And I want to bring kindness to others. I'm definitely happy to find righteousness and honor along the way. But instead of only focusing on those rewards, I'd really rather concentrate on living a life that pleases You and blesses the people You bring across my daily path. I admit that some days I'd rather not be very righteous or kind at all. But deep down, I want to do all these things for Your glory, Lord! In Jesus' name I pray, amen.

Here I Am, Lord

The LORD called Samuel. Samuel answered,
"Here I am." And he ran to Eli and said, "Here I
am; you called me." But Eli said, "I did not call;
go back and lie down." So he went and lay down.
1 SAMUEL 3:4–5 NIV

God, I thank You that You chose to call Samuel, who was just a boy, to serve You. Just as You called Samuel, I believe You still call Your people—Your *young* people!—to know You and to serve You. Lord, I am listening for Your voice. Even if it's not audible to others, I believe that You speak to my heart. God, teach me how to serve You today. Like Samuel, I am eager and ready to respond by serving You with joy and faithfulness. Speak, Lord. Amen.

God of All Comfort

Blessed be the God and Father. . .
of mercies and God of all comfort.
2 CORINTHIANS 1:3 NKJV

· ·

You comfort me, Father, when my heart aches. When everything in my life seems to be going wrong and when everything in the world seems to be going wrong too, Your comfort never fails. Thank You for offering me that constant care in my life. Help me share Your comfort with others—ultimately leading them to You.

Sin Be Gone

He does not deal with us according to our sins,
nor repay us according to our iniquities.
For as high as the heavens are above the earth,
so great is his steadfast love toward those who
fear him; as far as the east is from the west, so
far does he remove our transgressions from us.
PSALM 103:10–12 ESV

Father, sometimes my sin feels sticky—like gum on my shoe. Maybe it's a sin that feels too big for You to forgive. Or one that I commit and confess to You again and again. I'm tempted to believe that those sins are still clinging to me. But Your Word promises that the sins I've confessed to You are *gone*. They've been completely removed. Today I hold on to that truth. Lord, thank You for Your grace that is bigger than I can imagine! Amen.

Honoring My Parents

Children, obey your parents in the Lord,
for this is right. "Honor your father and
mother"—which is the first commandment with
a promise—"so that it may go well with you and
that you may enjoy long life on the earth."
EPHESIANS 6:1–3 NIV

. . . .

Father, I have heard Your instruction to honor my parents—both in the Old Testament's Ten Commandments and in Paul's letter to the church in Ephesus. I hear You, Lord. Your Word clearly says that I am to respect, love, and honor my parents. Sometimes that's really easy, but sometimes I struggle to obey Your Word. God, be my Helper as I purpose to honor my parents—with my attitude, with my words, and with my actions—so that You may be glorified. Amen.

Obedience Leads to Joy

"If you keep my commands, you will remain in my love, just as I have kept my Father's commands and remain in his love."
JOHN 15:10 NIV

. . . .

Lord, Your Word says that if we obey Your commands, we will remain in Your love. I want to serve You from an obedient heart. Just as Jesus submits to You, Father, I choose to submit to You too. Empower me, encourage me. Help me want to make decisions that lead to joy.

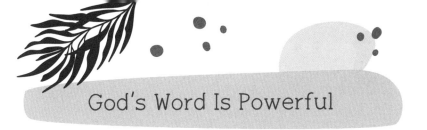

God's Word Is Powerful

The word of God is alive and powerful. It is sharper than the sharpest two-edged sword, cutting between soul and spirit, between joint and marrow. It exposes our innermost thoughts and desires.
HEBREWS 4:12 NLT

• •

I can't hide from You, Lord. You know *everything.* Although You love me as I am, the Bible—Your Word that's living and active and so powerful—helps me see what's wrong in my life. Thank You for Your grace that enables me to repent and change.

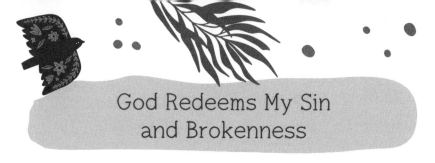

God Redeems My Sin and Brokenness

"Neither this man nor his parents sinned,"
said Jesus, "but this happened so that the
works of God might be displayed in him."
JOHN 9:3 NIV

. . . .

Lord, the idea that first-century people assumed that a man had been born blind because his parents had sinned, or because he'd sinned, seems like such antiquated thinking. It almost seems absurd. And yet at times part of me believes that some people are responsible for their own suffering. Or even that I am responsible for suffering that I don't and can't control. Yet Your Word reminds me that You are redeeming a broken world. So I offer You my hurting places, my broken places, and my sinful places so that Your power may be displayed in my life for Your glory. Amen.

Bearing Fruit

The fruit of the Spirit is love, joy, peace,
forbearance, kindness, goodness,
faithfulness, gentleness and self-control.
Against such things there is no law. Those
who belong to Christ Jesus have crucified
the flesh with its passions and desires.
GALATIANS 5:22–24 NIV

Gracious God, I notice a tug inside me between what You've designed me for and what my flesh wants: pleasure, entertainment, distraction, satisfaction. Because I feel the pull and want to be faithful to You, I will water the seeds You have sown in my heart so that the fruit of Your Spirit might flourish in me. Let Your love, joy, peace, patience, kindness, goodness, faithfulness, gentleness, and self-control live in me and through me. May others who see my life taste and see that *You are good*! Amen.

No Record of Wrongs

*[Love] does not demand its own way. It is not
irritable, and it keeps no record of being wronged.*
1 CORINTHIANS 13:5 NLT

· ·

I can't seem to help myself, Lord. I have this list in
my mind of all the things people have done to hurt
me. I can't seem to let it go. Help me give up keeping
score. Help me not to bring up the past over and over
but rather to let love erase all these wrongs.

I Will Hear

"Before they call I will answer;
while they are still speaking I will hear."
ISAIAH 65:24 NIV

. . . .

Dear Lord, I praise You for being the God who hears. I praise You that You know my heart better than *I* do. I can relax because You are answering my prayers before I even finish praying. Help me be more like You by listening with love to the people around me. I need Your ears and Your heart, Lord. Amen.

Safe and Protected

I love you, O LORD, my strength. The LORD is my rock and my fortress and my deliverer, my God, my rock, in whom I take refuge, my shield, and the horn of my salvation, my stronghold. I call upon the LORD, who is worthy to be praised, and I am saved from my enemies.
PSALM 18:1–3 ESV

• •

O Lord, I do love You! It's such a relief to know that You are my strength, my rock, my fortress. When I'm in trouble, You'll help me. Even when it's obvious that I have enemies—whether bullies verbally or physically threaten me—I know You'll save me. You're my protector, and for that I praise You! I'm thankful I can completely put my trust in You and call upon You at any time. As I fall asleep tonight, I pray I can rest peacefully, knowing that You care about me and protect me moment by moment. In Jesus' name I pray, amen.

A Godly Confidence

*Now this is the confidence that we
have in Him, that if we ask anything
according to His will, He hears us.*
1 JOHN 5:14 NKJV

. . . .

Dear Lord, sometimes it feels like my prayers are just
a long list of wishes and You're some sort of genie. I'm
so thankful that's not true. You don't give me what
I want just because I want it. You give me only what
lines up with Your will. Help me see what that is.

Call to Me

*"Call to me and I will answer you and tell you
great and unsearchable things you do not know."*
JEREMIAH 33:3 NIV

• •

Father God, You know everything. You see everything.
You are everywhere all the time. Sometimes we think
we are so smart. Compared to You, though, we are
babies one minute old, not understanding *anything*.
You want us to grow up. You want to teach us what You
know. So here I am, giving You my mind, Lord. Amen.

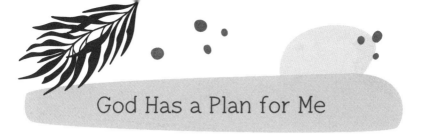

God Has a Plan for Me

*I know the plans I have for you, declares
the LORD, plans for welfare and not for
evil, to give you a future and a hope.*
JEREMIAH 29:11 ESV

God, some days it feels as if the future stretches out in front of me, but I can't see what it looks like. Some of my friends have a clear sense of what they want to study and what job they want to do one day. But when adults ask me what I want to do or be when I get older, I don't know for sure. Help! Today I take comfort in Your promise that You have a plan for my good. And that is enough. Today I take a deep breath and place my trust in You. Amen.

You Hear My Cry

Hear my cry, O God; listen to my prayer.
From the ends of the earth I call to you, I call
as my heart grows faint; lead me to the rock
that is higher than I. For you have been my
refuge, a strong tower against the foe.
I long to dwell in your tent forever and take
refuge in the shelter of your wings.
PSALM 61:1–4 NIV

God, sometimes I feel like I am all alone. Even my family and friends don't seem to understand me completely. And so I turn to You. You have always been there for me when I've needed You in the past, and I trust that You are with me and for me today. God, when I'm with You, I feel safe and protected. I know, in my deepest places, that You hear my cry and listen to my prayer. And You care. Amen.

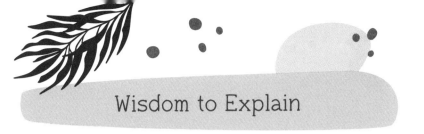

Wisdom to Explain

*Work hard so you can present yourself to God
and receive his approval. Be a good worker,
one who does not need to be ashamed and
who correctly explains the word of truth.*
2 TIMOTHY 2:15 NLT

. . . .

Lord, I want to please You. Teach me how to live so
that I receive Your approval. Give me a hunger for
reading the Bible so I'll know it better, and help me
share what I learn. I want to be a person who correctly
explains the Word of Truth.

A Good Work

*For I am confident of this very thing,
that He who began a good work in you
will perfect it until the day of Christ Jesus.*
PHILIPPIANS 1:6 NASB

. . . .

Father, sometimes I look at my life and it doesn't feel like there are many good things in it. My relationships are confusing. Life feels like a mess and so unlike the way I wish it was. But I absolutely trust You and am overwhelmed by the fact that You've begun a good work in me. In me! And by faith, I know You'll finish that good work until it's complete. I don't have to worry about perfecting what You're doing because You're the One who began the work and will continue perfecting it. Please help me to not get in Your way. Please open my eyes so I can see some of the good works You're accomplishing in me and through me. In Jesus' name I pray, amen.

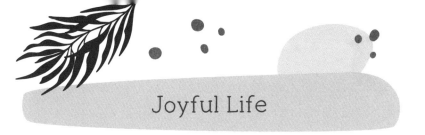

Joyful Life

You will go out with joy, and be led out in peace.
ISAIAH 55:12 NLV

· ·

Lord, thank You for the joy You bring to my life. Joy is with me because You are with me! May all creation—even the trees—praise You as I praise You. Help me live with a light heart and a positive attitude, despite the distractions and responsibilities that try to bring me down. I choose You. I choose to go through each day with joy.

Make Me Wiser

*If any of you lacks wisdom, you should ask
God, who gives generously to all without
finding fault, and it will be given to you.*
JAMES 1:5 NIV

• •

Father God, I found myself in a tricky situation today.
I want to do Your will, but first I need Your wisdom.
I'm not Solomon—the wisest man who ever lived—but
just like he did, I'm asking for Your wisdom. Thank
You that You promise to give it to me generously.

Being a Friend in Hard Times

A friend loves at all times, and a brother
is born for a time of adversity.
PROVERBS 17:17 NIV

· ·

God, I thank You for the friends whom you have placed in my life. I receive my friends from church, from school, and from my neighborhood—and maybe even faraway friends from camp or from a town where I used to live—as good gifts from You. It's been easy to love my friends when we're having fun, and when we're thriving. But I ask You to teach me how to love my friends well when their lives are difficult: when they lose a loved one to death, when their parents are separating, when they're forced to move, when their sibling is ill, or when they face other challenges. God teach me to be that friend who is faithful in adversity. Amen.

Called God's Daughter

*You have not received a spirit that makes you
fearful slaves. Instead, you received God's Spirit
when he adopted you as his own children. Now we
call him, "Abba, Father." For his Spirit joins with
our spirit to affirm that we are God's children.*
ROMANS 8:15–16 NLT

• •

Father, because I am human, I see the ways that I
am a slave to sin. If I'm keeping it real, sometimes I
enjoy wrongdoing for a while, but it always becomes
a cruel master. And yet what is *most true* about me
is that, through Jesus, You have set me free from the
power of sin and death by adopting me as Your own
daughter. And when I call You *Abba*, Father, my spirit
agrees with Your Spirit that I belong to You. Thank
You that Your love that sets me free is stronger than
the slavery of sin. Amen.

God's Great Love

*See how very much our Father loves us, for he
calls us his children, and that is what we are!*
1 JOHN 3:1 NLT

A good father protects his children. He loves his children unconditionally. He understands and forgives his children. He provides for his family. Lord, You are so much more than a good father—You are the *perfect* Father. Remind me that *this* is the way You love me. Thank You for loving me completely and perfectly.

Please Forgive Me

I do not understand what I do. For what I want to do I do not do, but what I hate I do.
ROMANS 7:15 NIV

• •

Father, I have sinned against You today—and I really, really regret it. I wish I weren't so quick to sin. I wish I could obey You, and I wish I could make good decisions. Tomorrow, please help me honor You moment by moment in what I think, say, and do. Please help me live a righteous life—not in a holier-than-thou, judgmental sort of way toward my friends and family. But in the hidden places of my heart, please help me live the kind of life that reflects You as my Lord. I want to be authentic and live for You, not for myself. In Jesus' name I pray, amen.

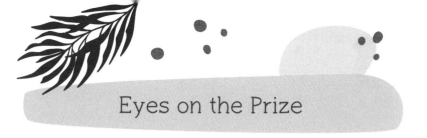

Eyes on the Prize

*My eyes are on the crown. I want to win
the race and get the crown of God's call
from heaven through Christ Jesus.*
PHILIPPIANS 3:14 NLV

. . . .

Father God, so many distractions fight for my attention—my phone, clothes, sports—but I want to use my time and energy wisely. The most important thing in my life is knowing You and living for You. I need Your help here, Lord. I can't keep my eyes on the crown like this verse says without You!

Being Made New

If anyone is in Christ, the new creation has come: The old has gone, the new is here!
2 CORINTHIANS 5:17 NIV

. . . .

Lord, I thank You for Your promise that anyone who is in Christ is being made new. Because that's me, God! And yet, when I look at my life, I recognize so much of the old self still hanging around. I notice the ways I act when I'm in a bad mood. I see how I can treat people poorly. I recognize the ways I'm loose with my language. And I'm aware of the ways I'm tempted, daily, to sin. But because I trust in Your promise, I offer myself to You today, so I may be *made new*. I know I can't make myself into a new creation, so I trust in the work of Your Spirit in my life. Amen.

The Most Important Thing

Hear, O Israel: The LORD our God, the LORD is one. Love the LORD your God with all your heart and with all your soul and with all your strength. These commandments that I give you today are to be on your hearts.
DEUTERONOMY 6:4–6 NIV

. . . .

God, as I navigate the waters of my life—at home, at school, and in the community—I need a rudder. And when I look to Your Word, I discover that You have given a clear directive that helps me steer through all I am facing. Your words in Deuteronomy tell me what Jesus later confirms: the most important thing is loving You with all my heart, all my soul, and all my strength. This is my rudder today. Amen.

To Know God's Will

We continually ask God to fill you with the knowledge of his will through all the wisdom and understanding that the Spirit gives.
COLOSSIANS 1:9 NIV

• •

Lord, I want to know Your will for my life. Please give me understanding. Show me when to stay and when to go, when to speak and when to close my mouth. Help me see Your best for me—right now and in the future. And help me accept Your answers obediently and joyfully.

Believe and Love

This is his command: to believe in the name of his Son, Jesus Christ, and to love one another as he commanded us. The one who keeps God's commands lives in him, and he in them. And this is how we know that he lives in us: We know it by the Spirit he gave us.
1 JOHN 3:23–24 NIV

. . . .

Lord Jesus, I believe in Your name, and I want to do what You've commanded. I pray Your Spirit will clearly direct me and help me live out Your commands in everyday life. You lived a life of love; I want to do the same, even if and when it's not easy. Please help Your love be obvious in my life and in the way I treat everyone around me. Even when I need to deal with the unlovable or people who are downright mean, please help me choose to love them. Thank You for Your love and for the way it completely changed my life and future. Thank You, also, for Your Spirit, and for the way He is proof that You live in me. In Your name I pray, amen.

Doing the Right Thing, the Right Way

*Do everything without grumbling or arguing,
so that you may become blameless and
pure, "children of God without fault in a
warped and crooked generation." Then you
will shine among them like stars in the sky
as you hold firmly to the word of life.*

PHILIPPIANS 2:14–16 NIV

. . . .

Lord, I thank You for calling me Your child. I want to live like I belong to You. Sometimes, even when I obey my parents or follow You, I do it with a grudging heart. I do the right thing but with the wrong attitude. But my aim is to be blameless before You. God, change my heart so that I can do all things to Your glory. I want to shine like a star in the sky for You. Amen.

Revive Me!

The law of the LORD is perfect, refreshing
the soul. The statutes of the LORD are
trustworthy, making wise the simple.
PSALM 19:7 NIV

. . . .

Lord, sometimes life gets crazy. I get so tired and stressed out from school and sports and chores. I can't wait to sit in Your presence and be refreshed. Revive my soul with Your Word. Dunk me in Your truth. Turn the dark places in my life to light so I can radiate Jesus everywhere I go.

You Promise to Answer

*"Call to me and I will answer you and tell you
great and unsearchable things you do not know."*
JEREMIAH 33:3 NIV

. . . .

Gracious Father, I thank You that Your Word assures
me that You see me, You hear me, You know me, and
You love me. God, I confess that sometimes when I
pray, I feel like I'm talking to the ceiling. It's hard for
me to believe that my little prayers are reaching Your
ears. And yet I hear You inviting me to pray, and I believe, deep inside me, that You are listening. Not only
do You hear, but You also promise to answer me. God,
that is hard for me to wrap my mind around! When I
pray, teach me to listen for and to recognize Your still,
small voice—and sometimes loud one—that answers
my prayers. Amen.

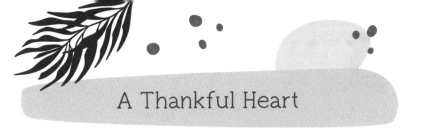

A Thankful Heart

*Rejoice always, pray continually, give
thanks in all circumstances; for this is
God's will for you in Christ Jesus.*
1 THESSALONIANS 5:16–18 NIV

Lord, You are my God, and I'm glad to give You the deepest part of me: my heart. Transform my heart so it's a joyful, thankful one. I want to be a girl who prays and makes a difference in her world. Lord, today, right where I am, I say thank You!

Good Gifts

"So if you sinful people know how to give good gifts to your children, how much more will your heavenly Father give good gifts to those who ask him."

MATTHEW 7:11 NLT

. . . .

Lord, I'm just a teenager, but I know what's a good gift and what's not. You are a loving and generous Father, and You know how to give good things better than anyone else. You give us so much! Lord, thank You for giving only good things when we ask.

In God I Trust

Some trust in chariots and some in horses,
but we trust in the name of the Lord our God.
PSALM 20:7 ESV

. . . .

Father God, when I look around me every day, I see people trusting in all sorts of things—money, power, grades, friends, clothing, social media likes, and themselves. But why trust in any of that? What can those things do? If they aren't fleeting—and so many of them are—they're powerless. I don't want to trust in the things of this world. I don't want to get caught up in obsessing over something that's just temporary. And I certainly don't want to trust in myself. But I trust You. I trust that You have all power and authority. I pray I'll continue to rest in You when I'm tempted to shift my eyes and attention on myself or on trivial things. Thank You that You're trustworthy! In Jesus' name I pray, amen.

God Is Love

*God is love. Whoever lives in love
lives in God, and God in them.*
1 JOHN 4:16 NIV

. . . .

Dear God, You are love—patient, kind, not envious, not proud, not rude, not self-seeking, not easily angered. You keep no record of wrongs. You're not happy about evil, but You rejoice in the truth. You always protect, trust, hope, and keep going. Your love will always remain. It is the greatest thing there is! May I always make my home in Your love.

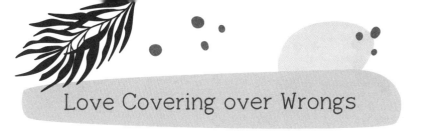

Love Covering over Wrongs

Hatred stirs up conflict,
but love covers over all wrongs.
PROVERBS 10:12 NIV

God, I thank You that You know the name and face and heart of every person I will meet this day. You know which ones love me and have my back, and You also know which ones are likely to attack, wound, or hurt me or others. So I offer every interaction to You, God. Teach me, especially how to love those whose words and behavior are unlovely. Dispel any hatred in my heart, so that I might be a vessel that channels Your great love for them. May my love function like beautiful paint that covers an ugly graffiti wall, obliterating any hint of wrong. Not in my strength—obviously!—but in Yours, and to Your glory. Amen.

When I'm Low, He Lifts Me Up

*I waited patiently for the LORD; he turned to me
and heard my cry. He lifted me out of the slimy
pit, out of the mud and mire; he set my feet on
a rock and gave me a firm place to stand.*
PSALM 40:1–2 NIV

. . . .

Lord, You know there are days when I am low—
emotionally, spiritually, physically. There are days
when I feel like I am sinking, stuck in a muddy pit,
and I can't get out. But even in the pit, I know I'm not
alone. You see me. You hear me. You help me. And,
like the psalmist, sometimes I have to wait. And even
though I want relief *right now*, I know that You are
reliable, and You are with me. God, I'm counting on
You to put my feet—my flip-flops, my sneakers, my
boots, my heels—on solid ground. Amen.

Give Me Joy

The Laws of the Lord are right, giving joy to the heart. The Word of the Lord is pure, giving light to the eyes.
PSALM 19:8 NLV

. . . .

Lord, Your words make my heart joyful, and joy is something everybody needs. I might be happy or I might not be happy, but Your joy sticks around no matter what I'm going through or feeling. Thank You for Your joy, Lord. Thank You for Your Word that is a bright light in my life.

Here I Am!

*Then I heard the voice of the Lord saying,
"Whom shall I send? And who will go for
us?" And I said, "Here am I. Send me!"*
ISAIAH 6:8 NIV

. . . .

Father, You are awesome. Before anything was, You were. You spoke absolutely everything into existence. And You had and still have a plan for everything and everyone. Even me. Sometimes I wonder if You can ever use me to do Your work or do great things for You. But as long as I listen to Your direction, obey, and do Your work, You can and will use me. That's amazing! I pray You'll give me strength and courage to step out and do Your work. When there's fear in my heart, please give me courage. When I doubt what I should do, please give me clarity. When I'm tempted to stick to what's comfortable, please help me choose obedience over all. Here I am. Send me. In Jesus' name I pray, amen.

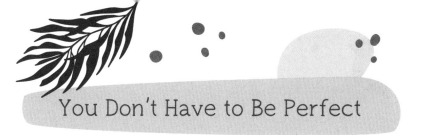

You Don't Have to Be Perfect

For the law was given through Moses;
grace and truth came through Jesus Christ.
JOHN 1:17 NIV

. . . .

Lord, when I struggle with perfectionism, help me break free! I know wanting things to be done right can be a good thing, but it can go too far. I want to live in Your grace. Keep me from judging myself too harshly and from fearing how others judge me. Help me see that because of Your grace, I am good enough.

The Power of Surprising Love

If your enemy is hungry, give him food to eat;
if he is thirsty, give him water to drink.
In doing this, you will heap burning coals on
his head, and the LORD will reward you.
PROVERBS 25:21–22 NIV

God, You know the enemies I'm facing right now. You know the people in my life who tear me down instead of build me up. I need Your help, and I thank You for Your clever and holy strategy to defeat them! You haven't given me a weapon of violence, but one of love. And You promise that when I extend love and good gifts to my enemy, I am *winning*. Today I will take You at Your word, and I will confound my enemy with love. In Your name and to Your glory, amen.

Because God Loved Me, I Love

Dear friends, since God so loved us,
we also ought to love one another.
1 JOHN 4:11 NIV

• •

Father in heaven, teach me to love like You do. I want to show Your love to those around me—my parents, my siblings, my friends, my classmates, and even strangers. But it can be hard! It's hard when others are being difficult. It's hard when I'm low on resources. It's hard when love requires sacrifice. And yet that costly kind of love is exactly what Jesus offered to the world—and offers to me. When I look at the life of Jesus—His words, His actions, His relationships—I know exactly what Your love is like. And because He loved me, I commit to offering others the same love. Amen.

Words to Live By

*Study this Book of Instruction continually.
Meditate on it day and night so you will be
sure to obey everything written in it. Only then
will you prosper and succeed in all you do.*
JOSHUA 1:8 NLT

Father, I respect Your Word. I want to give it first place in my life. The Bible is like my umpire, sorting out problems and answering questions that come up every day. Help me remember that when my actions spring from Your Word, things go well.

Sharing the Good News

*For I am not ashamed of the gospel
of Christ, for it is the power of God to
salvation for everyone who believes.*
ROMANS 1:16 NKJV

- -

Dear Father God, I'm not always patient about waiting
for things. But You are patient, Lord. You are waiting.
You are waiting for *us*. You won't return until everyone
has had a chance to hear the Gospel. Who can I tell,
Lord? Who is near me who hasn't heard or understood
the Good News?

No Drifting

We must pay the most careful attention,
therefore, to what we have heard,
so that we do not drift away.
HEBREWS 2:1 NIV

Father God, I'm so glad I've heard Your truth. Not only have I heard it, but I fully believe it and want to be obedient to You and Your Word. I want to follow You. I don't want to drift away. Even when I feel pushed and pulled to be more like the world, I want to be more like You. I don't want to fall into the trap of doing things to fit in with my friends. And I don't want to do what's popular if it doesn't line up with Your truth. Please help me bravely live for You. Keep me close to You, and show me what Your good, pleasing, and perfect will is for my life. In Jesus' name I pray, amen.

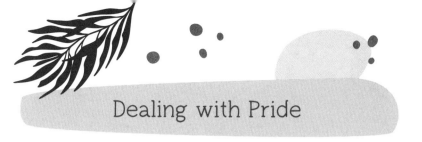

Dealing with Pride

Do not think of yourself more highly than you ought, but rather think of yourself with sober judgment, in accordance with the faith God has distributed to each of you.

ROMANS 12:3 NIV

. . . .

Lord, help me not to be prideful or arrogant; but when I am, please forgive me. Humble me, Lord, and lift me up so I'm a willing servant. With my eyes on You, not on myself, may I see the needs that other people have and help them.

The One Who Truly Satisfies

Jesus declared, "I am the bread of life. Whoever comes to me will never go hungry, and whoever believes in me will never be thirsty."
JOHN 6:35 NIV

. . . .

Father, everything within me hungers for life that really is life. And yet I regularly fill my heart, mind, and body with that which does not satisfy. I fill my ears with a constant stream of music; I fill my eyes with media feeds, shows, and movies; I fill my body with whatever tastes good and makes me feel good. Forgive me, Lord. Feed me with Yourself, for You are the only thing that satisfies my hunger and my thirst. I feast on You and on Your Word, and I am finally full. Amen.

Putting on the New Self

You were taught. . .to put off your old self,
which is being corrupted by its deceitful desires;
to be made new in the attitude of your minds;
and to put on the new self, created to be like
God in true righteousness and holiness.
EPHESIANS 4:22–24 NIV

. . . .

God, I know that I am Yours and that I'm being transformed to look more like You. And in that process, I reflect the image of Christ. So I am taking off the old, dirty, ill-fitting clothes and behaviors that used to be mine. Cleaned up, I'm being transformed to look more like You. Lord, clothe me in Your righteousness and holiness, so that others can see You in me. Today I choose to discard the old and put on the new. Amen.

Wisdom and Might

*"Blessed be the name of God forever
and ever, for wisdom and might are His."*
DANIEL 2:20 NKJV

. . . .

Lord, You are wise. I'll never grasp the vastness of Your knowledge and insight, but I'm thankful to have Your wisdom in my corner. Scripture says that along with being wise, You are powerful too. No matter how strong and mighty we humans think we are, You are the One who has *all* the power. Today I'm relying on Your wisdom and might.

For Rainy Days

*My voice You shall hear in the morning,
O LORD; in the morning I will direct
it to You, and I will look up.*
PSALM 5:3 NKJV

· ·

Lord, it's so dark this morning. I don't want to be in this gray light. I just want to be where You are. I want to be with You, walking on streets of gold. I can't wait for endless days of glory in heaven. Lord, please shine Your love and light on my heart today.

All My Heart

*Trust in the LORD with all your heart and
do not lean on your own understanding.
In all your ways acknowledge Him, and
He will make your paths straight.*
PROVERBS 3:5–6 NASB

. . . .

Father, I know I can be completely honest with You because You know what word I'll say before it's even on my lips. So when I tell You that I struggle with trusting in myself, it comes as no surprise to You. The fact is that I do lean on my own understanding. I try to figure things out on my own. I try to set my own course and live my own way. But Lord, I need You. I need to trust You with all of my heart. I need to lean on Your understanding. I want to acknowledge You in all of my ways because You are the living God. It's a bonus that You'll make my paths straight and help make sense of my life. I believe this. Please help me stop trying to direct my own life and instead live out my belief in You. In Jesus' name I pray, amen.

Sit Down and Rest

Do you not know? Have you not heard? The LORD
is the everlasting God, the Creator of the ends
of the earth. He will not grow tired or weary.
ISAIAH 40:28 NIV

. . . .

Lord, I'm so amazed by You, especially by the fact that
You never grow tired. I do get tired. I need a break
right now! As I sit with You tonight when everything
is quiet, help me be still. Help me rest well so that
tomorrow I am strong again.

"Fear Not, for I Am with You"

*Do not fear, for I am with you; do not
be dismayed, for I am your God. I will
strengthen you and help you; I will uphold
you with my righteous right hand.*
ISAIAH 41:10 NIV

. . . .

God, I thank You that there is no moment of my
life—past, present, or future—in which You have left
me alone. In every hurt, in every joy, in every disappointment, in every surprise, *You are with me.* God,
impress this transforming truth upon my heart and
mind. When I'm taking tests, when I'm playing sports,
when I go to the doctor, when I sit in church, when I
hang with my friends, You are strengthening me and
helping me. God, thank You that You never leave me
nor forsake me. Amen.

He Makes Me Lie Down

The LORD is my shepherd, I lack nothing.
He makes me lie down in green pastures,
he leads me beside quiet waters,
he refreshes my soul.
PSALM 23:1–3 NIV

· ·

Although I know You invite me to rest, Lord, I find myself filling my time with all sorts of commitments and distractions. I give myself to school, to clubs, to sports, to activities, to service, to church, and to youth group. And then, if I have a free moment, I become absorbed in my phone, my laptop, or the television. God, I find it hard to be still. And yet I hear the gentle voice of my Shepherd inviting me to pause. To stop. To rest. God, You invite me to lie down in lush grass and stretch out beside quiet waters. Help me to pause. To stop. To rest. Amen.

Peace

Grace and peace to you from God the Father.
2 THESSALONIANS 1:2 NIV

. . . .

Thank You, Father, for Your peace. Help me remember that Your peace is the only true rest for my soul—and that I should always run to You and no other idol in my life. When troubles come my way, please give me an extra dose of Your peace. And when I see others who are upset, help me say or do something that will encourage them to seek out Your peace.

The Cheerleader

I can do all things through
Christ who strengthens me.
PHILIPPIANS 4:13 NKJV

. . . .

Dear Lord, in this verse I can hear You cheering me on. What can I do? *All things!* Who's going to help me? *Christ!* What's He going to do? *Strengthen me!* I thank You for bringing these particular words to me right now. I know I'm going to need this verse today, Lord. Help me repeat it in my heart all day long. Amen.

Weighed Down

But You, O LORD, are a shield about me,
my glory, and the One who lifts my head.
I was crying to the LORD with my voice,
and He answered me from His holy mountain.
PSALM 3:3–4 NASB

. . . .

Father, tonight I come to You weighed down by life.
I cry out to You—literally crying about what's going
on. You know the details. You know what burdens my
heart. You know what I can't get off my mind. Even
in all of my despair, frustration, and sadness, I pray
I'll rest in the way You're my shield of protection. You
and You alone are my glory—my excellence! You lift
my head as it's heavy with tears and exhaustion. I am
so thankful I can come to You for comfort. I praise
You for Your goodness and Your never-ending love
for me. Thank You for listening to my prayers and
answering them. I love You so very much. In Jesus'
name I pray, amen.

Confidence

The LORD will be at your side and will
keep your foot from being snared.
PROVERBS 3:26 NIV

Lord, help me have more confidence—not in myself but in You. I don't want to be arrogant, but I don't want to be a doormat either. Give me a teachable heart. You have so much to show me, and I want to learn Your ways. Learning and growing, I am alive! Full of Your Spirit, I can stand confident and strong.

Serving Like Jesus

*Who, being in very nature God, did not
consider equality with God something to be
used to his own advantage; rather, he made
himself nothing by taking the very nature of
a servant, being made in human likeness.*
PHILIPPIANS 2:6–7 NIV

. . . .

Every voice around me, Lord, is lobbying me to do
more, achieve more, play more, and win more. And
I confess that I'm tempted—on application essays, at
parties, and in interviews—to make myself appear to
be more than I really am. And yet, in Your Word, I am
relieved of the pressure to seem big and important.
Instead, imitating Jesus, I can aim to be smaller by
serving others the way He did. Father, give me Your
heart to imitate the posture of Jesus by stopping to
serve others, in Your name. Amen.

Known and Called

The word of the LORD came to me, saying,
"Before I formed you in the womb I knew
you, before you were born I set you apart;
I appointed you as a prophet to the nations."
JEREMIAH 1:4–5 NIV

- -

God, when I turn to Your Word, I see the way You called all kinds of unlikely people. You called a young boy named David, who became king, and a teenage girl named Mary, who gave birth to Jesus. You surprised everyone with Your unlikely choices! And even though Jeremiah thought he was too young and didn't have the right words, You called him to be Your prophet. God, I also believe You knew me and called me when I was still in my mother's womb. Help me pay attention today to the ways You want to use me to build Your kingdom. Amen.

Waiting on God

LORD, I wait for you; you will answer, Lord my God.
PSALM 38:15 NIV

. . . .

I feel like I'm standing at a starting line, Lord, ready to run. All I need is Your signal for me to go. I think I've figured out what I need to do in this situation and I'm ready to do it, but I know I need to wait for Your timing. Help me be patient. Show me when and how to follow Your plan for me.

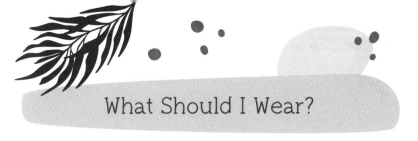

What Should I Wear?

"Why are you worried about clothing? Notice how the lilies of the field grow; they do not labor nor do they spin thread for cloth, yet I say to you that not even Solomon in all his glory clothed himself like one of these. But if God so clothes the grass of the field, which is alive today and tomorrow is thrown into the furnace, will He not much more clothe you?"

MATTHEW 6:28–30 NASB

Father, in Your Word, Jesus promised that I don't have to worry about the clothing I wear. That is so different than the focus of the world. But just like You clothe the lilies of the field so beautifully, You'll clothe me too. I pray You'll help me be content with what I wear and that I'll modestly protect my body. Please help me see the wonderful ways You actually do bring outfits and clothing into my life—ways that I don't have to worry about or consider. Thank You for faithfully and generously providing for all my needs and so many of my wants. You are so good to me! In Jesus' name I pray, amen.

A Person of Wisdom

Blessed are those who find wisdom, those who gain understanding, for she is more profitable than silver and yields better returns than gold.
PROVERBS 3:13–14 NIV

• •

Lord, I want to be a person of wisdom, not foolishness, because wisdom is what enriches my life. Help me make right choices and behave in a way that is worthy of Your name. I pray that I would be honest and upright every day so my actions reflect You and Your ways.

Reconciled to God and Others

"If you are offering your gift at the altar and there remember that your brother or sister has something against you, leave your gift there in front of the altar. First go and be reconciled to them; then come and offer your gift."
MATTHEW 5:23–24 NIV

. . . .

Lord, I want to honor You by living well. I want to worship You with my whole heart. And yet when I have sinned against others, I cannot love You with my whole heart. When I've hurt someone in my family, or when I've said something unkind to a friend, I cannot love You like I want to. So quicken my mind to see if there are any against whom I've sinned. Open my eyes to notice from whom I might need to ask forgiveness. And give me the courage to humbly confess and ask forgiveness, so that I might be right with them and with You.

When I'm Down and When I'm Up

Is anyone among you in trouble? Let them pray. Is anyone happy? Let them sing songs of praise. Is anyone among you sick? Let them call the elders of the church to pray over them and anoint them with oil in the name of the Lord.
JAMES 5:13–14 NIV

. . . .

Lord, You know how I am. When things are going great, I am happy to zip along without a nod of thanks to You. And when I'm struggling, when my life is in pieces, I'm the first person to bang on Your door. But I hear You calling me to something different, inviting me into *more*. Yes, You invite me, and others in Your body, to come to You when we're in trouble. Done! And You also invite us to turn to You when we're happy and when we're sick. God, quicken my heart and mind to bring everything in my day before You. Amen.

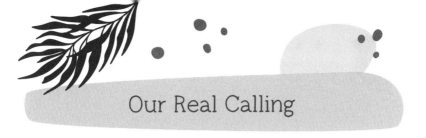

Our Real Calling

We told you with strong words that you should live to please God. He is the One Who chose you to come into His holy nation and to share His shining-greatness.
1 THESSALONIANS 2:11–12 NLV

Lord, whatever job I have when I'm an adult, I know my true calling is pleasing You. You chose me! And now I want to live in a way that both shows my thanks to You and shows other people who You are. Amen.

Chosen by You

He predestined us to adoption as sons through Jesus Christ to Himself, according to the kind intention of His will, to the praise of the glory of His grace, which He freely bestowed on us in the Beloved.
Ephesians 1:5–6 nasb

. . . .

Father, I admit that I don't understand Your plans or Your choices. But even when I can't understand something, I can still appreciate it. So tonight I thank You for choosing to adopt me. You could choose absolutely anyone (and You do!), so to know that You've chosen *me* is amazing. You are so kind, and Your will reflects Your kindness. I praise You and Your grace, and I thank You for giving it to me so generously through Jesus. I don't deserve it, but even so, I pray I might start living my life in a way that is worthy of You and Your gift—and that I'll never take You for granted. In Jesus' name I pray, amen.

The Construction Site

*Being confident of this, that he who began
a good work in you will carry it on to
completion until the day of Christ Jesus.*
PHILIPPIANS 1:6 NIV

Father God, I'm a work in progress. Sometimes I feel like there should be construction tape around my rough edges. I'm not who I want to be, and I'm not who You want me to be *yet*. You love me anyway. Thank You for the sure promise that You are working in me.

God Shoulders My Worries

*"Can any one of you by worrying
add a single hour to your life?"*

MATTHEW 6:27 NIV

God, when I start worrying—about schoolwork, about my commitments, about the future—I feel so alone. I carry this heavy burden of worries that only stresses me out. And yet when I listen to the gentle words of Jesus, I'm reminded that You care for me. You already know the things I'm worrying about, and You invite me to trust You with them. Just as You care for the birds of the air and the flowers of the field, just as You meet their needs, You meet my needs. I can see that worrying doesn't change one thing! Good Father, today I release my anxieties, my concerns, and my worries to You. And because I trust You, I receive Your gentle comfort.

One Who Delights over Me

*"The LORD your God is with you, the Mighty
Warrior who saves. He will take great delight
in you; in his love he will no longer rebuke
you, but will rejoice over you with singing."*
ZEPHANIAH 3:17 NIV

. . . .

God, I tip the eyes of my heart up toward heaven and
I look for Your face. Sometimes when I search for You,
I expect to see something that resembles the human
faces I've known: a face that's distracted, or absent,
or disappointed, or even angry. But that is not Your
expression toward me. Instead, Your Word assures
me that You *delight* in Your people! You even rejoice
over us with singing! God, I have every confidence
that today You are with me. Help me see You clearly
so that I might receive Your great, great love. Amen.

Twenty-Four Hours

This is the day that the Lord has made.
Let us be full of joy and be glad in it.
PSALM 118:24 NLV

. . . .

I thank You for this day, Lord, with its twenty-four hours. Only twenty-four. Seems like I always cram so much into my day and then fall into bed exhausted each night. But how many hours do I give to You? Sometimes not even one! Help me give You more of each day, Lord, so we can be closer than ever.

Watch Yourself!

Brothers and sisters, if someone is caught in a sin, you who live by the Spirit should restore that person gently. But watch yourselves, or you also may be tempted.

GALATIANS 6:1 NIV

Father, I found out that one of my friends is sinning. The thing is, I don't know if my friend is even sorry. It almost seems like my friend is enjoying the sin. I'm upset by it—and I don't want to follow the same path. Could You please help me? I'd like to follow Your Word and try to gently help my friend get back to the right way. But I'm worried I'll be tempted in the process. Please keep me from temptation and from falling into the same sin. I love You and want to do what's right in Your eyes. In Jesus' name I pray, amen.

A Life of Love

"Love your neighbor as yourself."
MATTHEW 22:39 NIV

. . . .

Lord, I want to live a life of love! Show me what true love is—Your love—so I can receive it and give it away to others. Teach me to care for my neighbor as I would care for myself. Let love be my motivation. Help me speak kind, encouraging words and bless others with my actions. I thank You for Your amazing, unconditional, steadfast love for me.

Worries into Prayers

Don't worry about anything; instead, pray about everything. Tell God what you need, and thank him for all he has done.
PHILIPPIANS 4:6 NLT

. . . .

Lord God, I praise You for how You are changing me. I praise You for how You are teaching me to pray about my worries. I trust You. *You* are the overcomer; *You* are my resting place; *You* are my strength and my fortress. I am so relieved to give my worries to You and let them become prayers.

Death Does Not Win

"Death is swallowed up in victory." "O death, where is your victory? O death, where is your sting?" The sting of death is sin, and the power of sin is the law. But thanks be to God, who gives us the victory through our Lord Jesus Christ.
1 CORINTHIANS 15:54–57 ESV

· ·

Lord, I struggle to understand the power of death in the world. When I see tragedies in the news, or when someone I know has died, I wrestle to understand *why*. When someone's life is cut short, it feels as if death has won. But You promise that, in the end, death does *not* win. And when I look at the crucifixion, death, and resurrection of Jesus, I know that it is true. God, even though I don't fully understand, I trust that You are the great Redeemer. Amen.

Prioritize Prayer

"Blessed is the one who trusts in the
Lord, whose confidence is in him."
JEREMIAH 17:7 NIV

. . . .

Lord, I feel like a withered plant with dry, brown leaves. Help me connect with You in prayer so I can grow strong and healthy, inside and out, like a vibrant green tree. You are my source of living water. Teach me to be still, to listen, to absorb what You want to reveal to me as we talk one on one.

Full of God's Truth

Let the teaching of Christ and His words keep on living in you. These make your lives rich and full of wisdom. Keep on teaching and helping each other. Sing. . .with hearts full of thanks to God.
COLOSSIANS 3:16 NLV

· ·

Lord, fill my heart and mind with the words of the Bible, and help me share what I've learned with others so their lives can be rich too and so we all can sing to You with thankful hearts.

Bullied

*But the salvation of the righteous is from the
LORD; He is their strength in time of trouble.
The LORD helps them and rescues them.*
PSALM 37:39–40 NASB

· ·

Father God, I'm so glad You're for me, because it feels like so many people are against me. The bullies in my life seem so wicked. They plan and do and say such horrible things. Please help me remember that You don't see me the same way they do, and most people don't see me that way either. I pray You'll be my strength when it doesn't feel like I have any. When I'm in trouble, please help me. Keep me safe from these bullies. I want to grow closer to You in this awful time—I run to You for help because I feel so helpless. I pray You'll bring something good out of these bad situations and help me shine Your light even when I don't feel like it. Instead of getting back at mean people, please help me treat them with undeserving love, just like Jesus did. In His name I pray, amen.

I Need Jesus

On hearing this, Jesus said, "It is not the healthy who need a doctor, but the sick. But go and learn what this means: 'I desire mercy, not sacrifice.' For I have not come to call the righteous, but sinners."
MATTHEW 9:12–13 NIV

· ·

Lord, when I go to school or church, I'm around people who give the impression that they don't even need You. On the outside, they look like they've got it all together. And so I try to act like that too. But when I'm honest with myself and with You, I know that I need You. And You confirm my suspicion when You say that You came for sinners. God, that's me! So I come to You, not as someone who's healthy and strong, but as someone who is sick and needs Your healing. Receive me, Lord, today. Amen.

Speaking to God Throughout the Day

*Rejoice always, pray continually,
give thanks in all circumstances; for this
is God's will for you in Christ Jesus.*
1 THESSALONIANS 5:16–18 NIV

. . . .

God, I thank You for the assurance I have that You are with me and for me. I confess that too often I zip through my day with little thought of You. Forgive me. God, I want to notice Your presence with me throughout today. When I eat with my family, when I spend time with my friends, when I work on assignments or at my job, when I encounter strangers on the street, I want to recognize You in every one of those moments. And Your Word invites me to welcome You into each one by praying continually. God, help me to converse with You in my heart—speaking and listening—throughout this day.

Anything Can Happen

"What do you mean, 'If I can'?" Jesus asked.
"Anything is possible if a person believes."
MARK 9:23 NLT

. . . .

Father God, You are so amazing! When You first saved me, I felt like the world had shifted under me and anything was possible. The knowledge that You did miracles (and might for me too) made me feel like I was beginning a new kind of life that would be beautiful and grand. It's not just a feeling, Lord. Anything *can* happen. I praise You for this truth!

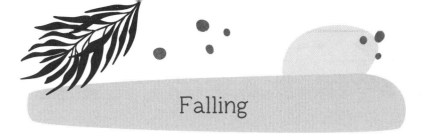

Falling

Give all your cares to the Lord and He will
give you strength. He will never let those
who are right with Him be shaken.
PSALM 55:22 NLV

Lord, it's been a tough day. I'm worried about so much, it's exhausting. So I'm going to follow Your advice and give my cares to You—every last one. Tonight I'm falling into Your arms for the comfort and strength I need. I know You will take care of both my worries and me.

Gotta Have Faith

*Faith is confidence in what we hope for and
assurance about what we do not see.*
HEBREWS 11:1 NIV

• •

Father God, I come to You tonight but admit that
sometimes I don't always know You're real. When You
seem so quiet, it's hard to remember that You're the
living God. I want to believe in You. I want to worship
the one true God. Please help me keep my faith in
You. Even when I don't feel like You're there, please
help me remember that faith is not a feeling, and the
truth of Your existence doesn't depend on whether I
can see or feel or hear You. You are there. You are real,
living, and You are at work in the world today. Thank
You for loving me even when I'm tempted to doubt
You. In Jesus' name I pray, amen.

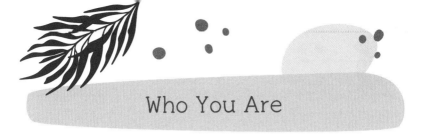

Who You Are

God wants these great riches of the hidden truth to be made known to the people who are not Jews. The secret is this: Christ in you brings hope of all the great things to come.
COLOSSIANS 1:27 NLV

. . . .

Dear Jesus, help me find my identity in You, not the world. As I read the Bible, help me understand who You created me to be. Point out the true identity that is mine through my relationship with You.

Act, Love, Walk with God

He has shown you, O mortal, what is
good. And what does the Lord require
of you? To act justly and to love mercy
and to walk humbly with your God.

MICAH 6:8 NIV

. . . .

After You delivered Your people out of Egypt, Lord, they strayed from Your ways. And like a loving Father, You yearned for them to return to You. You even made it plain to them what You were asking them to do: to act justly, love mercy, and walk humbly with You. Father, although I wish I were better than they were, I recognize my heart in theirs. And I hear You calling me to honor You with my life in the same way. So embolden me to be a person who acts justly. Soften my heart so that I love mercy. And teach me what it means to walk humbly with You. Amen.

You Know Me Inside and Out

My frame was not hidden from you when I was made in the secret place, when I was woven together in the depths of the earth. Your eyes saw my unformed body; all the days ordained for me were written in your book before one of them came to be.

PSALM 139:15–16 NIV

• •

Father, I thank You that You know me inside and out, and that You love me. Lord, I'm convinced that You know exactly what is happening in my life. You know the disappointment I felt yesterday. You know the challenge I'm battling today. And You know what I will face tomorrow. Nothing in my experience is hidden from You. None of it is a surprise. Lord, thank You that, in all things, You are with me and You are for me. Amen.

I Am God's Child

*The Spirit of God, who raised
Jesus from the dead, lives in you.*
ROMANS 8:11 NLT

Dear Jesus, thank You for providing the way for me to belong to Your family. I am a child of God, and You are my Elder Brother and my example. I will do my best to follow in Your footsteps. I want to be like You, Lord. I want to have the same character. Thank You for including me in the greatest family ever!

Spirit-Led

*For those who are led by the Spirit
of God are the children of God.*
ROMANS 8:14 NIV

. . . .

Heavenly Father, let Your Spirit lead me in everything.
Let me always look to You for guidance. Keep me from
the temptation to listen to what the world says I should
be or do. Forgive me when I ignore Your Spirit. Help
me tune in to Your Holy Spirit so that I hear Your voice
every day in each decision and each action.

Seek Peace and Pursue It

Whoever of you loves life and desires to see many good days, keep your tongue from evil and your lips from telling lies. Turn from evil and do good; seek peace and pursue it.
PSALM 34:12–14 NIV

. . . .

Heavenly Father, sometimes it's so tough to live in peace with other people. But even when I see conflict all around me, I want to choose peace. I want to do good. I want to let Your peace shine through my life. When people are stressed and worried, please help me be a peaceful influence. In the heat of the moment, help me to remember that my mouth has a lot to do with keeping peace. I know the words I choose have influence and power. I pray You'll use me and my words to calm people down in a gentle, kind way. Where there's trouble, I don't want to add to the conflict by what I say or do. Please use me as a peacemaker. In Jesus' name I pray, amen.

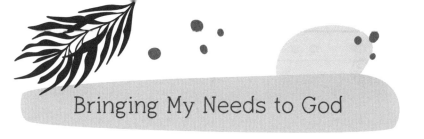

Bringing My Needs to God

"What do you want me to do for you?"
Jesus asked him. The blind man said, "Rabbi,
I want to see." "Go," said Jesus, "your faith
has healed you." Immediately he received his
sight and followed Jesus along the road.
MARK 10:51–52 NIV

• •

Jesus, I believe You are the Great Physician who heals bodies and souls. Thank You, Lord. I confess, though, that sometimes I hesitate to ask You for what I most need. Instead I wrestle to manage on my own and do not ask for Your help. Forgive me, Lord. Today I am bold to bring my needs to You, confident that You listen and that You care. I ask for Your help, and I wait with patience and expectation to see what You will do. Amen.

God Bless My Home

The LORD's curse is on the house of the wicked,
but he blesses the home of the righteous.
PROVERBS 3:33 NIV

Lord, please bless my home. I ask for Your protection to be here with me and my family. Fill each room with Your presence, Your peace, and Your power. May my whole family treat each other with respect and kindness. Use this house in ways that glorify You, Lord. And may anyone who comes here feel at home.

Pleasing Just One

Am I now trying to win the approval of human beings, or of God? Or am I trying to please people? If I were still trying to please people, I would not be a servant of Christ.

GALATIANS 1:10 NIV

. . . .

Lord, You know my heart. And You know how tempting it is for me to want to please people. I want my parents to be proud of me. I want my peers to like me. I want teachers, bosses, and coaches to think highly of me. And those aren't bad things! But when my need for human approval trumps my longing to please You, I am missing the mark. First and foremost, I am a servant of Christ. And today I commit my heart to please You above all others. Be my helper, in Jesus' name and for His sake. Amen.

God Shepherds His Flock

He tends his flock like a shepherd:
he gathers the lambs in his arms and
carries them close to his heart.
ISAIAH 40:11 NIV

. . . .

Lord, I have a friend who's hurting. She needs someone right now, and I'm not sure I can be that someone. I know You care for us like a shepherd taking care of his flock of sheep. Please gather my friend in Your arms, and carry her until she's not hurting anymore.

Live Worthy

As a prisoner for the Lord, then, I urge you to live a life worthy of the calling you have received.
<small>EPHESIANS 4:1 NIV</small>

. . . .

Lord, I'm not locked in jail like the apostle Paul was, but I'm enslaved by my love for You—a really great thing! You've called me to believe in You, and I take that call seriously. I want to live a life worthy of my calling, like the Bible says. Thank You for helping me. (I know You will!)

Different Than the World

*But Noah found favor in the eyes of
the LORD. . . . And Noah did all that
the LORD had commanded him.*
GENESIS 6:8; 7:5 ESV

. . . .

Lord God, You have such a wonderful way of not only
knowing Your children but also caring for them. You've
proven this time and again in my life and in Your Word
through stories like Noah's. Even though Noah lived in
a wicked, wicked world, he still honored and obeyed
You. In fact, he did everything You commanded him,
no matter what others around him said or did. And
when he followed You, he found favor in Your eyes.
Just like Noah, many days it feels like I'm living in a
wicked world. I pray that even if my obedience to You
makes me completely different than everyone else
around me, I'll obey anyway. I want to follow You and
do all that You command me to do. I want to trust You
and You alone. It's my heart's true desire to find favor
in Your eyes. I love You and want to honor You every
day of my life. In Jesus' name I pray, amen.

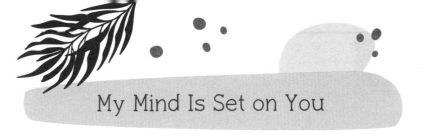

My Mind Is Set on You

You will keep in perfect peace those whose minds are steadfast, because they trust in you. Trust in the LORD forever, for the LORD, the LORD himself, is the Rock eternal.
ISAIAH 26:3–4 NIV

God, I turn to You today for help. My heart and mind and body are busy, and what I most need is Your peace. I read in Your Word that You give peace to those who trust in You, whose minds are steadfast. Lord, today I need Your help to fix my mind on You. Keep me from turning to shallow distractions, false substitutes that cannot satisfy my deepest desires. God, help me to keep my mind fixed steadfastly on You, my Rock Eternal. Amen.

Flowing with the Seasons

To everything there is a season, a time
for every purpose under heaven.
ECCLESIASTES 3:1 NKJV

. . . .

Lord God, I know there is a season for everything. The Bible tells me there is a time for every purpose under heaven—a time to weep, a time to laugh, a time to mourn, and a time to dance. Help me recognize the season I'm in and flow with it. Show me how to bend as You lead the way.

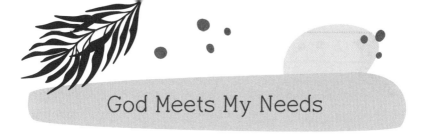

God Meets My Needs

Keep falsehood and lies far from me;
give me neither poverty nor riches, but give
me only my daily bread. Otherwise, I may have
too much and disown you and say, "Who is
the LORD?" Or I may become poor and steal,
and so dishonor the name of my God.
PROVERBS 30:8–9 NIV

God, You are my faithful provider, and I trust You to meet my needs. I confess that when I feel like I don't have what I think I need, I spend a lot of time and energy thinking how I can get it! And when I'm honest, I admit that there is a lot I want that I really don't need. You know my heart. God, I believe that You are my good Provider, and I trust that I don't need everything I want. Above all, I want to honor You. Amen.

The God Who Saves

O God Who saves us, help us for the honor of Your name. Take us out of trouble and forgive our sins, for the honor of Your name.
PSALM 79:9 NLV

God, You are the only One who can save me and keep me safe forever. No one else—not even the people who love me—can do that. If I start to trust in other people or things when I'm stressed and insecure, point me back to You—the God who saves.

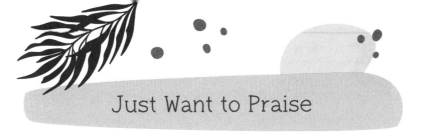

Just Want to Praise

*"Then you will have joy in the All-powerful,
and lift up your face to God."*
JOB 22:26 NLV

. . . .

Father God, today I just want to praise You! You are awesome, You are holy, You are merciful. You saved me! You are all that is good, Lord, and You are almighty. You made *mountains*. And trees that reach into the sky and birds as bright as rainbows and flowers so perfect and beautiful. Who is like You? No one compares to You. Amen and amen and amen.

A Living Hope

Praise be to the God and Father of our Lord
Jesus Christ! In his great mercy he has given
us new birth into a living hope through the
resurrection of Jesus Christ from the dead,
and into an inheritance that can never perish,
spoil or fade. This inheritance is kept in heaven
for you, who through faith are shielded by
God's power until the coming of the salvation
that is ready to be revealed in the last time.

1 PETER 1:3–5 NIV

God and Father, thank You for Your mercy that I don't deserve. And thank You for hope that is real and living. I look forward to what's waiting for me in heaven. It won't ever fade or spoil! Even though it may seem like a very long time until that's my reality, I can start looking forward to it. I'm thankful that in my every-day life You shield me with Your power and guarantee my future. I praise You for the way You care for me today and will continue to care for me forever. In Jesus' name I pray, amen.

Encouraging Words

Gracious words are a honeycomb,
sweet to the soul and healing to the bones.
PROVERBS 16:24 NIV

Lord, I pray that I would speak encouraging and kind words to my friends and family. Help me build others up—never tear them down. Help me not be so self-absorbed that I forget to ask how others around me are doing. May my words be positive. May they be sweet to the soul and healing to the bones—like honey!

Making New Friends

Live in harmony with each other. Don't be too proud to enjoy the company of ordinary people.
ROMANS 12:16 NLT

. . . .

God, I thank You for the crew of family and friends that You have given me. They are a gift and a blessing from You. God, I also want You to open my eyes to the ones whom this world marginalizes. Show me the people in my school, in my community, in Your larger world, and even at my church who are overlooked and undervalued. Help me to notice those from different cultures, with different abilities, the ones who are "other." Give me Your eyes to see them, Your heart to love them, and the commitment to enter into real friendship with them. Thank You, in advance, for the gifts they will share with me. Amen.

What Makes Heaven Rejoice

*I tell you that in the same way there will be
more rejoicing in heaven over one sinner
who repents than over ninety-nine righteous
persons who do not need to repent.*
LUKE 15:7 NIV

. . . .

Lord, I confess that sometimes I take my salvation for
granted. And yet when I listen to the stories that Jesus
tells, I remember that there is great rejoicing when
even one sinner repents. I believe that You delight in
me, and I believe that Your heart longs to see others
find You. God, let me be Your faithful witness today.
Show me one person who needs to know about Your
loving-kindness, and equip me to share Your Gospel
by my love, by my actions, and by my words. Amen.

Planning Ahead

Ants—they aren't strong,
but they store up food all summer.
PROVERBS 30:25 NLT

· ·

Lord, my life gets so busy, sometimes all I can see is today. Remind me to lift my head and look up once in a while. I'm young, but I still want to think about what You might have in store for my future. Help me to set worthy goals and to fix my eyes on You so I can see where we're going together and the plans You have for me.

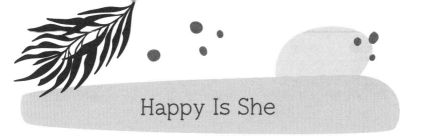

Happy Is She

*Where there is no understanding of the
Word of the Lord, the people do whatever they
want to, but happy is he who keeps the law.*
PROVERBS 29:18 NLV

• •

Lord, we'd be lost if we didn't have the Bible to show us how to live. But when we obey You, You work through us to bring Your good plans to completion. I can trust You whether things around me are going smoothly or not. Keeping Your commands and walking in Your blessings make me very happy!

Guard Your Heart!

Above all else, guard your heart,
for everything you do flows from it.
PROVERBS 4:23 NIV

Lord God, I know my heart is an important part of me that guides my thoughts and decisions. So often, this culture tells me to follow my heart. But sometimes I'm not exactly sure what I'm following. My feelings seem to go all over the place—every day they seem to change, and even moment by moment. Some days it feels like I'm on a wild roller-coaster ride. Instead of trusting my ever-changing feelings, I pray that I'll start to guard my heart more carefully. Please help me keep bad influences out and cling to the good influences that please You. Give me wisdom, Father, to know what needs to stay in my heart—and what things need to go. In Jesus' name I pray, amen.

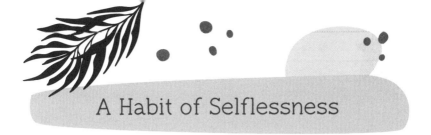

A Habit of Selflessness

Since Christ has suffered in His body, we must be ready to suffer also. Suffering puts an end to sin.
1 PETER 4:1 NLV

. . . .

Jesus, I've been self-centered. Sometimes I've felt like the world revolved around me. Forgive me for my selfishness. I won't die if everything doesn't go my way. Help me not to react so emotionally when things don't turn out as I expected them to. Help me think of others before myself, just as You thought about us.

Honoring God with My Body

Do you not know that your body is a temple of the Holy Spirit within you, whom you have from God? You are not your own, for you were bought with a price. So glorify God in your body.
1 CORINTHIANS 6:19–20 ESV

God, I give You thanks for the physical body You have given me. I know it's not *perfect*—in either its appearance or its function—but I believe that You knit me together and that my body is *good*. Voices around me try to convince me that it is mine to use as I please: eating whatever I want, drinking whatever I want, smoking whatever I want, and behaving however I want. And yet I also hear Your kind, gentle voice reminding me that my body is *where You live*! Teach me what that means and empower me to make choices that honor You. Amen.

It Was His Plan

God saved us and called us to live a holy life.
He did this, not because we deserved it, but because
that was his plan from before the beginning of
time—to show us his grace through Christ Jesus.
2 TIMOTHY 1:9 NLT

• •

Lord God, Your plan to save us wasn't random. You set it in motion from the very beginning! And I'm so thankful that it doesn't depend on us but rather on Your grace. Use me to bring other people to You.

Loving Fiercely

Ruth replied, "Don't urge me to leave you or to turn back from you. Where you go I will go, and where you stay I will stay. Your people will be my people and your God my God."

RUTH 1:16 NIV

• •

Father, when I read the story of Ruth, a single woman who was far from the home where she was raised, I am impressed by her relationship with Naomi—the mother of the husband Ruth lost. And even though Naomi released her to return to her own family, Ruth was dogged in her commitment to Naomi and to You. I don't see that kind of tenacity much today, God, but I want to be a young woman who is *fierce* in my love for You and for others. Strengthen me to love fiercely today. Amen.

Get Well Soon

Have mercy on me, LORD, for I am faint;
heal me, LORD, for my bones are in agony.
PSALM 6:2 NIV

. . . .

Father, I haven't been feeling very good lately. And I'm tempted to let that affect my moods and attitudes. I know all things happen for a reason, but, Father, I wish I didn't have to feel this way! I pray You'll heal me. Please restore my health and help me feel better. When I'm tempted to worry about what's wrong, please fill me with peace. When I want to complain about how I feel, please help me keep a good attitude. And I pray I could get plenty of rest and feel like myself again. In Jesus' name I pray, amen.

Sharing Challenges

*Be an example to all believers in what
you say, in the way you live, in your
love, your faith, and your purity.*
1 TIMOTHY 4:12 NLT

. . . .

Father God, You know everything I've been through
and all the ways I struggle. Help my life be an example to anyone who is going through the same things
or struggling in the same ways. I want to share how
I've trusted You in my challenges. Give me words to
encourage them to trust You too.

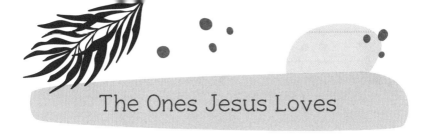

The Ones Jesus Loves

When Jesus reached the spot, he looked up and said to him, "Zacchaeus, come down immediately. I must stay at your house today." So he came down at once and welcomed him gladly. All the people saw this and began to mutter, "He has gone to be the guest of a sinner."
LUKE 19:5–7 NIV

. . . .

God, You know what my life is like. You know the pressures to be among peers who are popular, who are smart, who are socially savvy. And You also know the pressures I face to avoid being seen with those who are on the margins, who are awkward, who are looked down upon. And yet You made a beeline toward people like Zacchaeus who were avoided by those in their community! Today, Jesus, give me Your heart for those around me who have been marginalized. Amen.

Everlasting Word

*O LORD, You are my God. I will exalt You,
I will praise Your name, for You have
done wonderful things; Your counsels
of old are faithfulness and truth.*
ISAIAH 25:1 NKJV

• •

Dear God, the Bible is thousands of years old. How many books made that long ago are still useful today? I can't think of even one! Your Word is as true and helpful today as it was when the ink was wet. I'm so amazed and so thankful. Amen.

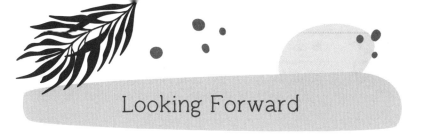

Looking Forward

"When the Spirit of truth comes, he will guide you into all truth. . . . He will tell you about the future."
JOHN 16:13 NLT

. . . .

Sometimes I look back at the things that didn't turn out quite right for me, Lord. I know I shouldn't focus on the past. You've set a great life ahead of me, and I want to embrace it wholeheartedly. Help me see the future with joy because my hope is in *You*!

Becoming a Do-Gooder

*And let us not grow weary of doing good, for in
due season we will reap, if we do not give up.*
GALATIANS 6:9 ESV

. . . .

Father God, sometimes it feels like I try so hard to do
good—to make life better for other people, to do my
best, to be a good example of what it's like to follow
You. But all of that goodness wears me out. I get tired.
I pray that even if I'm feeling weary, You'll give me
the strength to keep on keeping on. I don't want to be
a quitter. And I really don't want to give up and stop
doing good things. Please help me see even just a tiny
result of what my good works are accomplishing for
You in the people around me. I love You and I want to
serve You with my life. In Jesus' name I pray, amen.

You Lighten My Load

"Come to me, all you who are weary and burdened, and I will give you rest. Take my yoke upon you and learn from me, for I am gentle and humble in heart, and you will find rest for your souls. For my yoke is easy and my burden is light."
MATTHEW 11:28–30 NIV

God, I thank You that You notice when I'm tired. You see when I'm overwhelmed. And You care that I am weary. You know every burden I bear—at school, at work, at home—and You offer me respite. You invite me to come and be with You, and You offer to shoulder my burden alongside me. As I picture You beside me, I can feel my load lighten. Thank You that You are gentle, and thank You for giving me rest for my weary soul. Amen.

Winning When Tempted

*The devil said to him, "If you are the Son of God,
tell this stone to become bread." Jesus answered,
"It is written: 'Man shall not live on bread alone.'"*
LUKE 4:3–4 NIV

· ·

Some days, Jesus, I feel as if the devil is on my back.
I feel as if he is near and he is tempting me. And You
know what that is like. I take comfort in the knowledge that You faced the enemy, just as I do. And when
I keep my eyes on You, I can see my way out of the
bind. When You were tempted, You didn't depend
on Your own willpower. No, You were empowered by
God's Word. That was Your source of strength, Your
superpower. Today, Jesus, remind me of Your Word so
that, like You, I remain faithful to our Father. Amen.

Live What You Believe

Let the Holy Spirit lead you in each step.
Then you will not please your sinful old selves.
GALATIANS 5:16 NLV

Lord, forgive me when my choices don't line up with what I believe. Teach me Your ways, and help me understand Your instructions. I want my faith to affect every area of my life whether I'm at school or home or church. Pull me back when I'm tempted to pull away. Help me be faithful to You always.

God Is Near to Me

Lord, you have been our dwelling place throughout all generations. Before the mountains were born or you brought forth the whole world, from everlasting to everlasting you are God.

PSALM 90:1–2 NIV

. . . .

God, I long to be in Your presence and to experience Your nearness. And Your Word reminds me that You have been the dwelling place for Your people for centuries. You have invited us to live with You. And so as I look around my bedroom today, or as I walk through my school's hallways today, I know that You are there with me! You really do dwell with me. In Jesus, You made Your home among women, and men, and children, and today You live with me. Thank You for holding me close. Amen.

Why I Serve

"For the LORD searches all hearts and understands all the intent of the thoughts. If you seek Him, He will be found by you."
1 CHRONICLES 28:9 NKJV

Lord, we talk a lot about serving others at church. I like to volunteer, but sometimes I'm not sure if I'm serving because I want to help people or because I want to feel good about myself. Search my heart and show me why I serve. Help me serve You and others with the right spirit.

Making God's Name Known

Give praise to the LORD, proclaim his name;
make known among the nations what he has
done. Sing to him, sing praise to him; tell of all
his wonderful acts. Glory in his holy name; let
the hearts of those who seek the LORD rejoice.
PSALM 105:1–3 NIV

God, You are faithful. You have done so much good in my life and the lives of others. And so I long to tell others of Your faithfulness. God, equip me today to share news of Your goodness with others. Help me share with a friend in need how You've changed my life. Help me remind a family member that You are always faithful, even when we can't see what You're up to. And help me share with someone in need the reasons why You can be trusted. Strengthen me today to tell all the wonderful things You have done. Amen.

Created for Good Works

We are God's masterpiece. He has created us anew in Christ Jesus, so we can do the good things he planned for us long ago.
<small>EPHESIANS 2:10 NLT</small>

. . . .

Father God, You shaped me into the unique person I am today. You created me to do good works. Long, long ago, before I was born, You planned the things I would do for You. Give me the courage to do those things. Help me be brave even when the tasks are challenging.

I Have What I Need

"Why do you worry about clothes? See how the flowers of the field grow. They do not labor or spin. Yet I tell you that not even Solomon in all his splendor was dressed like one of these."
MATTHEW 6:28–29 NIV

. . . .

Jesus, You are wise. And when I listen to You teaching Your first-century followers about what it means to trust Your Father, and ours, I hear echoes of solid truth for my own life. When You exhort Your disciples to worry less about scrambling after clothes, food, and shelter, I hear You speaking to me! And even though my daily physical needs are met, I surf online shopping sites for my next outfit, I keep thinking about that yummy pint of ice cream in our freezer, and I noodle on how I want to redecorate my room. But today, Lord, I trust You as the good Provider for all I need.

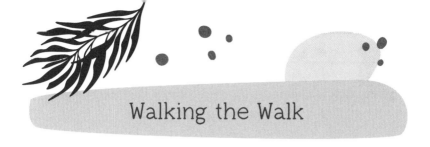

Walking the Walk

Therefore, as you have received Christ Jesus the Lord, so walk in Him, having been firmly rooted and now being built up in Him and established in your faith, just as you were instructed, and overflowing with gratitude.
COLOSSIANS 2:6–7 NASB

Father, thank You for Jesus. And thank You for His love for me. I believe He is Your Son who led a perfect life then died a cruel death on the cross. And I believe His death paid for my sins. Because I believe He is the only way, the only truth, and the only life, I boldly come to You through Him. I receive Christ Jesus as my Lord. I trust He has forgiven me of my sins. I pray that with this new life and forgiveness I would be rooted and built up in Him. May the things I think, say, and do every day be filled with faith and devotion to You. In Jesus' name I pray, amen.

My Perfect Father

*"Which of you, if your son asks for bread,
will give him a stone? Or if he asks for a fish,
will give him a snake? If you, then, though you
are evil, know how to give good gifts to your
children, how much more will your Father in
heaven give good gifts to those who ask him!"*
MATTHEW 7:9–11 NIV

. . . .

Father in heaven, I believe that You gave me parents to show me what Your love is like. Sometimes they reflect for me Your steadfast, faithful love. Other times, though, they fail to love me the way You do. But You assure me that Your love is of a higher order and that You delight in giving good gifts to those who ask You for them. Well, that's me. I am asking You to send the good gifts You have for me. Amen.

Together

Only let your manner of life be worthy of the gospel of Christ, so that whether I come and see you or am absent, I may hear of you that you are standing firm in one spirit, with one mind striving side by side for the faith of the gospel, and not frightened in anything by your opponents. This is a clear sign to them of their destruction, but of your salvation, and that from God.
PHILIPPIANS 1:27–28 ESV

Lord Jesus, I pray that my life will be joined to the lives of other believers. If I'm not letting believers into my life right now, please bless me with good relationships—mentors and friends who can help keep me close to You and who love You. I pray that through fellowship we can encourage one another to stand firm and strive for the faith of the Gospel. Please help us cheer one another on and not be scared of things in this world. Thank You that I don't have to face this Christian walk all on my own. Amen.

Serving from the Heart

As slaves of Christ, do the will
of God with all your heart.
EPHESIANS 6:6 NLT

· ·

Lord, I want to do Your will with all my heart and talent. I want to be a girl You can use to help other people. And I don't want to drag my feet—I want to be energetic about it! Help me focus on You and not on the talents You've given me. Help me understand what You've shaped me to do.

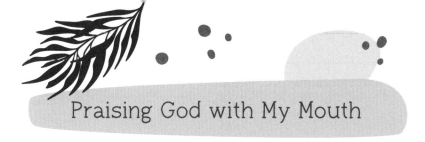

Praising God with My Mouth

Come, let us sing for joy to the L$_{ORD}$;
let us shout aloud to the Rock of our salvation.
Let us come before him with thanksgiving and
extol him with music and song. For the L$_{ORD}$ is
the great God, the great King above all gods.
PSALM 95:1–3 NIV

Good Creator, You are the Maker of all that is, and—
graciously!—that includes music. God, You know the
notes and chords and sounds that I pipe into my ears
every day. You know what makes my foot tap and
what makes my whole body dance. I receive music as
a good gift from You. And, God, I also want to return
my praise to You in song. I sing to You, and I join the
chorus of the faithful who thank and praise You with
melodies! You are the great God, and today I open my
lips to praise Your name. Amen.

Scripture Index

Inspiration and Encouragement for Your Heart

God Made You for More

Whether you're battling through a season of loneliness, heartache, disappointment, fear, insecurity, regret, shame, or unforgiveness, these 200 comforting, encouraging devotional readings will remind you that you were made for so much more.

Hardback / 978-1-64352-949-3

Mornings with God for Teen Girls

These 180 inspiring readings and prayers touch on topics important to your heart—like Positive Thinking, Confidence, Joy, Belonging, Trust, Hope, and so much more! With each turn of the page, you'll be gifted with a positive, faith-building message—guaranteed to start your day off right!

Flexible Casebound / 978-1-63609-616-2